It's Your Money.

The E*TRADE Step-by-Step Guide to Online Investing

Christos M. Cotsakos

HarperBusiness

An Imprint of HarperCollins*Publishers*

IT'S YOUR MONEY. The E*TRADE Step-by-Step Guide to Online Investing. Copyright © 2000 by Christos M. Cotsakos. All rights reserved. Printed in the United States of America. No part of this book may be used or reproduced in any manner whatsoever without written permission except in the case of brief quotations embodied in critical articles and reviews. For information address HarperCollins Publishers Inc., 10 East 53rd Street, New York, NY 10022.

HarperCollins books may be purchased for educational, business, or sales promotional use. For information please write: Special Markets Department, HarperCollins Publishers Inc., 10 East 53rd Street, New York, NY 10022.

FIRST EDITION

Produced by The Book Laboratory, Inc., Mill Valley, California
Designed by Victoria Pohlmann Design, Palo Alto, California
Graphic Production by i4 Design, Sausalito, California

Library of Congress Cataloging-in-Publication Data
Has been applied for.
Available upon request

ISBN 0-06-662003-1

00 01 02 03 04 10 9 8 7 6 5 4 3 2

"Get ready, get set, get online, go! Visionary industry leader Christos M. Cotsakos has written this excellent and straightforward guide for the next generation of online investors."

—Daniel H. Case III, Chairman and CEO, Chase H&Q

"*It's Your Money* is a must read for anyone interested in taking control of their financial future. A well written book with practical, easy to use strategies and tips to help investors capitalize on new online technologies to achieve their financial goals."

—Bob Emery, President and CEO, Robertson Stephens

"A pioneer in online financial services, Christos is truly passionate about educating and empowering the individual to take control of his or her finances. That passion is revealed throughout *It's Your Money*."

—John Metaxas, Anchor, CNN Financial News

"Christos was one of the few people that had the early vision of how the Internet could change the world and make it better. In this book he uses this vision to show how everyone can take advantage of the Internet to control their personal finances and improve their lives."

—Masayoshi Son, President and CEO, SOFTBANK Corporation

"Finally, a book I can recommend to the people who always ask me, 'How do I get started with investing?'. Finally, an objective handbook that takes into account everything you need to trade and invest online, from the computer and phone lines to fundamental and technical analysis. This is it, the only book you will need, to figure out how to get control of your finances and beat the professionals at their own game. My hat's off to Christos, he's done it again, put more financial power into the hands of the individual than anyone in the brokerage game. You want to get started? What are you waiting for, buy this book!"

—James J. Cramer, Co-founder, TheStreet.com

Inspired by William A. Porter, my friend and colleague,
founder of TRADE*PLUS, the forerunner of
E*TRADE, and leading entrepreneur of the
online investing revolution.

• • •

Dedicated to the global community
of empowered consumers,
our shareowners and partners who believe in our vision,
and my bodacious colleagues at E*TRADE
who make it happen 24 x 7 x 366.

Contents

Step IV: You've Got the Power

Step V: High Gear

Welcome
to the
Revolution

O ver the past four years, more than 15 million people made a choice—to be part of an extraordinary future that's unfolding around us. The Internet is creating a fundamental lifestyle change that's empowering us as individuals in ways we could not have imagined just a few years ago. The power and convenience of the Internet is revolutionizing how we communicate, work, and play. It will significantly impact how you earn, invest, protect, and enjoy your money.

At E*TRADE, we're living and reinventing the revolution every day. So it's easy for us to forget that, as I write this, nearly 94 percent of people in the world don't own a computer, including almost 33 percent of Americans. In fact, over 50 percent of U.S. households aren't even online yet.

That's why I've tried to write a fundamental and straightforward book about investing and managing your money online—to help you through the process. I've tried to remember what it was like to not even own a computer, to not be connected to the Internet, to not know how to manage my own money online.

As we forge ahead at E*TRADE, we want to make sure

> " What matters
> most is who you
> have in the foxhole
> with you when *they*
> yell...incoming! "
>
> Christos

everyone can participate in this revolution. There can no longer be the "haves" and the "have-nots"; we cannot allow a digital divide to separate us. We need to do whatever we can to make sure everyone has the opportunity to take advantage of the knowledge and power of the Internet. We want to help put choice and control in the hands and minds of individuals just like you.

We believe in you. You can and do make the difference in your own financial future. There's never been a better time to make your money work for you.

Sincerely,

Christos M. Cotsakos
Chairman of the Board and
Chief Executive Officer
E*TRADE Group, Inc.

*Note: Throughout this book, you'll see quotes from E*TRADE customers talking about their personal experiences with online investing.*

Step I:
Get
Ready

CHAPTER 1

Your Financial Future Is Online

That's not a dream or a promise or a myth, it's a fact. Every minute, another 19 people go online for the first time. In just seven years, we've gone from "What's the Internet?" to "You're not on the Web yet?" Thousands of new Web sites open every day. New connections. New pathways. New ways of understanding the world around you. If you're not already online, I'd like to help make you one of those 19 new users very shortly.

Like the automobile and the telephone, the Internet will fundamentally change the way our world works. In the same way that computer chips have made our cars smarter, our houses more convenient, and even our appliances easier to use, the Internet will make *all of us* smarter in nearly every area of our lives. And our personal finances will be no exception. Innovations in the ways in which money is transacted, invested, and monitored are at the forefront of this change.

Every day, more and more financial services and information are available to anyone with a computer, an Internet connection, and the desire to take control of his or her own financial future. In the second half of 1999, online transactions accounted for nearly 50 percent of all retail consumer

> **❝** The more you do online, the more success you have, and the more you get a boosted sense of self-esteem. **❞**
>
> S. B., Research Technician

investment transactions in the United States. It's the way the world is going.

Are those people who are already online and taking advantage of this revolution smarter than you? I don't think so. They just have access to the right tools and information. I believe if someone provided you with the basics—showed you how to use the tools and tap into the information that's out there—you could enjoy the power and freedom of investing and managing your money online, too. I'd like to help show you the way.

Do you like money? Good, you're normal. So, here you are at the start of a new millennium with nothing but opportunity in front of you. For you to miss out on this revolution would be unjustifiable—and there's no reason why you should.

Think about this:

Sitting in front of your computer, connected to the Internet, you have the power to be smarter and more in control of your money than virtually anyone at any time in the history of the world. Nearly everything you need to make informed investment decisions is a mouse-click away. Financial information on just about every company, government security, and investment instrument in the world is available to anyone on the Net with a little knowledge of what to look for.

The Internet is the single greatest public source of knowledge and information in the history of humankind. Economic reports? On the Internet. Trends and forecasts? On the Internet. Real-time stock quotes? On the Internet. Access to global financial markets? On the Internet. Extended-hours trading?

OH, WHAT TANGLED WEBS WE WEAVE

The Internet is a general term for a group of interconnected networks that enable computer users around the world to connect with each other and any other point on the network. Although there are technical differences, most people use several words interchangeably to refer to this grid. So do I: Internet, World Wide Web, the Web, the Net, and online.

Home Tech 2000

U.S. Homes	
95%	have Telephones
98%	have TVs
66%	have Cable access
60%	have PCs
50%	are Online

Data Forecasts: U.S. Census Bureau, Kagan Associates, Jupiter Research

On the Internet. Graphs. Charts. Numbers. Reports. Articles and commentary. A good online financial service provider will give you, free of charge, powerful research and analysis tools to examine potential investments. A great financial service provider will allow you to manage all your savings and investments with just a couple of mouse clicks, show you how your entire financial portfolio is performing at any moment in time, and send you an alert when there's a significant price change in a stock you're watching.

> **GETTING THERE IS HALF THE FUN**
>
> Are you uncomfortable with some of the terms I'm using? That's why I wrote this book: to give you the background and knowledge you need to start mining all the data that's available and to understand the process so you can start taking control of your financial future online. Stick with me. We're diving right into the twenty-first century.

Historically, investing in stocks has been the best way to significantly build your capital over a long period of time. Look it up. The younger you are, the longer the growth and the better the return. If you're in your 20s, single, without a kid or date on the horizon, then you've got a lot longer to build your capital than us 50-something baby boomers. Stock prices can fluctuate a lot over the course of a few days or a few years. But over the longer term, stock prices have indisputably risen in line with a company's profits and outlook.

Getting online and taking control of your own finances has never been more *affordable*. The Internet is driving down the cost of everything, and managing your money is no exception. The Internet levels the playing field by giving everyone online access to essentially the same information. And by making information more democratic, it creates downward pressure on fees.

> **THE DISCLAIMER**
>
> Our lawyers had a fit when they heard I was writing this book and insisted we insert the following disclaimer. You need to read this, because it's not just legal gobbledygook, it's important information you should think about before investing in *anything*.
>
> Past performance is not a guarantee of future results nor is it necessarily a guide to future performance. The investments or strategies presented may not be suitable for all investors. It is important that you consider the information in this book in the context of your personal risk tolerance and investment goals.

You can find the best price and the best rates on just about every product, service, financial instrument, investment opportunity, or anything else you're looking for. That's the power and freedom that comes with online investing.

Shopping around is the best way to get the best deals.
The bank around the corner doesn't always have the best
mortgage rates or even the best CD rates. The investment
instruments available through your compa-
ny's retirement plan possibly aren't the best
game in town. If you look around and do
your research, chances are you can find
better prices and more choices—if only
you knew where to look.

**Getting online and taking control of your
finances has never been *easier*.** Do you
seriously think anyone would build a con-
sumer-oriented online investing and banking
business and then *not* make it user-friendly?
Online financial sites have invested millions
to make it understandable and easy to
use. You don't need a degree in computer
programming or economics to understand
online investing. You just need a little
common sense and the willingness to learn.

LOOKS GOOD TO ME

Throughout this book, I'll show you
examples of how simple the mechanics
of online investing can be by showing
you samples of E∗TRADE's Web site.
If you explore other online financial
services, you'll probably find something
similar, and possibly just as clear and
easy to use. E∗TRADE, however, has
consistently won awards for our ease of
use and accessibility. Gomez Advisors,
Lafferty Information and Research
Group, *PC Magazine*, and *Smart
Computing* (to name a few) at various
times have cited E∗TRADE as having the
most user-friendly investing Web site in
the industry. I also use E∗TRADE's Web
site as an example because, frankly,
it's the site I know the most about and
naturally the site I'm most comfortable
discussing.

**Getting online and taking control of your
finances has never been *safer* or *more secure*.** The U.S.
Securities and Exchange Commission (the "SEC") and the
National Association of Securities Dealers Regulation
(NASDR) closely monitor the financial services industry.
The SEC is the federal watchdog that oversees the
exchanges, brokers, dealers, and certain investment advisors
to protect the public from malpractice, misfeasance, and
all the other mals and misses the government can think of.
The NASDR regulates both broker/dealers and the
NASDAQ stock market. Because online investing is so
new and evolving so quickly to meet investor demands,
I believe online financial companies may be even more
closely watched than traditional financial companies.

What about online security? Let me tell you how it
works at E∗TRADE: All online account transactions and

communications are secured through industry-leading **server authentication** and **data encryption**. Access to your account requires a personal ID and password, and you need to enter an additional transaction password before you can place a trade or move money. Online investing and banking at E*TRADE is as safe as—maybe safer than—placing a credit card order over the phone.

You're not alone. There are millions of people out there just like you: self-directed investors hunting for other points of view, ideas they can research immediately, or information on promising new strategies. Online, you have access to discussion groups, chat forums and investment clubs, both physical and virtual. At E*TRADE, our individual investors (first-timers and veterans) connect to one another through discussion groups, online forums, e-mail, and instant messaging to exchange ideas, tips, and information as part of their decision-making process.

Help is available. Most online financial service providers offer personal assistance. At E*TRADE, for example, we've got in-house customer service reps, technical support experts, and **registered representatives** available 24 hours a day, seven days a week, 366 days a year via a toll-free number. In addition, we've structured our Web site so that most questions can be asked and answered online. Ask us a direct question in plain English and you'll probably be shown the answer you're looking for. It's just a smart way to do business.

I believe that once you understand the basics of online investing, you can take more control over your own financial future. The technology is understandable. The information is accessible. The knowledge is attainable. The process is affordable.

server authentication
Ability to verify the source of information sent over the Internet.

data encryption
A method for securely passing information in an encoded format over the Internet.

registered representative
A person who is authorized to handle securities transactions.

I HEARD IT THROUGH THE GRAPEVINE
The Internet is the new frontier of free speech. Instantly, anonymously, anyone can say anything at any time. But in an arena where you can't meet face-to-face, you have to use some common sense. Who is this guy? Does he know what he's talking about? Are her motives legit? Could she be my sister-in-law? At E*TRADE, we're extremely vigilant and protective of our discussion groups and chat forums. Any hint of illegality and you're history. But that doesn't relieve you of your responsibility to think when you're on the Net. A healthy degree of discretion and skepticism is essential for assessing the wealth of information available to you.

Ready to take charge of your financial future?

Good. Let's get started.

How to Use This Book

If you don't own your own computer, keep reading.

If you own a computer, but aren't online yet, you can skip ahead to Chapter 3.

If you're already online but don't have an account with an online financial service provider, start at Chapter 4.

And if you already have an account with an online financial service provider but want to learn more about online investing and banking, you can go straight to Step III.

Talk to Me

Got questions? Take notes as you go through this book. If you have questions, send an e-mail to *itsyourmoney@etrade.com*. I'll see that someone answers any questions you might have.

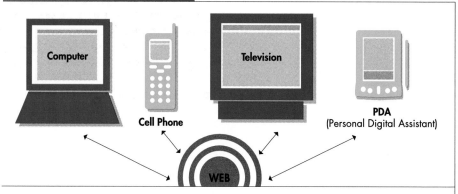

Web-enabled Devices

Computer

Cell Phone

Television

PDA
(Personal Digital Assistant)

WEB

Going, Going, Gone! Is the desktop computer a thing of the past? Companies are developing new technologies that are changing the way people get online, with PDAs (personal digital assistants), e-mail on your cell phone or pager, and the Web on TV. Whatever it is, you can be sure it'll be more efficient, more affordable—and designed to make your life easier.

Step II:

Get Set,
Get
Online

CHAPTER 2

Turn On,
Tune In

The Top Line

CHOICES, CHOICES

Very soon, you'll have a lot more to choose from than just the Mac or PC. Companies like Oracle, Intel, and Sun are introducing the *Net computer*, a relatively low-cost device designed just for accessing the Internet. Some of these devices run on Linux, an increasingly popular software system that operates the computer's basic functions. These new machines are designed to get you "turned on and tuned in" in seconds.

Y ou don't need to know how a car works in order to drive. And you no longer need an engineering degree to use a computer. Virtually every new computer today comes equipped with everything you need to connect to the Internet.

For the most part, the only significant decision you've got to make is Mac or PC— shorthand, of course, for Macintosh and Personal Computer (classically known as IBM-compatible). They're two different, essentially incompatible systems, like Beta and VHS. Everyone has an opinion about which one is better. Want my opinion? The one you start with is the one you're going to think is better.

Whichever system you choose, here's my "no-brainer-read-no-further" advice on getting a computer. Take the following information to your local retailer (or ask a friend to help you shop online) and you can be on the Internet tonight.

Do you need to know what all this means? No—but

I'll explain it later anyway. Do you have to follow this advice exactly? No—this is just a minimum suggested guideline (besides, all this is probably going to be out of date in a few months anyway).

For PCs (IBM-Compatible Computers):

300MHz processor (or higher). The processor has been called the motor or the brains of the computer. MHz, or megahertz, is a measure of the processor's oomph, sort of like horsepower.

At least 32MB of RAM. RAM stands for Random Access Memory. I like to think of RAM as room in the computer's workshop. The more room you have the bigger the jobs you can handle. I wouldn't go for less than 32MB; if you can afford more at the outset, go for it. In most of today's computers, you can add RAM later if you want more (and you will).

3GB hard-disk space. This is where you store the programs you use and the documents and data those programs create. GB stands for gigabyte, and that's a lot of storage space. These days, 1GB is the bare minimum.

17-inch monitor. Think of your TV screen. A 17-inch monitor gives you enough space to view the entire contents of most Web pages at once. For laptops or for the absolute minimum on a desktop, you can go down to 14 inches.

A printer. A simple black and white ink-jet printer will turn online data into paper "hardcopy" that you can read at your leisure or file away. Compare prices and take a look at how relatively inexpensive color printers have become.

Microsoft Windows 95 (or later). Windows is the basic operating software (OS) that runs the computer. All other programs you use will need the OS for their basic housekeeping chores. New computers will come with a later version of Windows, but Win95 is the minimum.

A modem running 56.6k (or faster). A modem is the basic hardware many people use to connect to the Internet. The k stands for kilobits per second and is a measure of the modem's speed.

A Web browser (software for navigating the Internet). I recommend using either Netscape Navigator version 4.6 or higher or Microsoft Internet Explorer version 4.0 or higher.

For Macintosh Computers:

(The terms are slightly different, but the information's the same.)

Macintosh G3 (this includes the iMac), with a 300MHz processor (or higher). The bare minimum Mac system is a PowerPC 7500.

At least 32MB of RAM. Again, I wouldn't go for less than 32MB; if you can afford more at the outset, go for it. All Macs let you add RAM later if you want more (and you will).

3GB hard-disk space. You need this space to store the programs you use and the documents and data those programs create. 1GB is the bare minimum.

A 15- or 17-inch monitor. A 17-inch monitor is preferable, but the iMac currently ships with a 15-inch display that is certainly acceptable. Your minimum laptop or desktop monitor size should be at least 14 inches.

> **THERE MUST BE A CATCH?**
> And with "free" computers, there is. New services have emerged that offer you a free computer or free Internet access. In exchange, they can monitor every click you make on the Web and push advertisements to you. If you're a real bargain hunter and don't mind the speed bumps, then this type of offering might be for you.

A printer. Check to make sure the printer you're buying has built-in compatibility with a Macintosh system. Some require additional hardware and/or software drivers.

Macintosh System 8.5 (or higher). This is the basic operating software (OS) that runs Macintosh computers and it's different from the Windows operating system. From your point of view, this is the main difference between Macs and

PCs, but virtually every important software program you would want is available for both Macs and PCs.

A modem running 56.6k (or faster). This is the basic hardware needed to connect your computer to the Internet.

A Web browser (software for navigating the Internet).
I recommend using either Netscape Navigator version 4.6 or higher or Microsoft Internet Explorer version 4.0 or higher. (Note: The version numbers are different for Macs than they are for Windows.)

If you're going to buy a new system, about $950 will get you into the game on the Windows side, a bit more for a Mac. Spending more than $1,500 should make you look like a computer whiz. When you go shopping, look for freebies—software that comes preloaded on the machine, for example—but don't let this stuff turn your head. The basic system architecture is what's really important.

Rather not pay for the whole thing up front? Hardware manufacturers are always coming up with new ways to make it easier for you to obtain the latest system. Some offer low monthly payment plans or their own lines of credit. Others are now offering leasing options to consumers. A knowledgeable friend can help you compare options online.

You should also pay some attention to warranties and free or prepaid technical assistance packages. Computer manufacturers aim for "plug and play" simplicity and most succeed, but if you have trouble, having strong technical support can be a big relief.

A computer retailer (online or offline) should be able to help you through the decision-making process. If the site or salesperson can't answer your questions in easy-to-understand everyday English, find one who can.

CASTING A WIDE CNET

Once you're online, you can continue your Internet education at any number of sites that cover computer technology and the Net. One of the best is CNET (*www.cnet.com*) providing the latest in high-tech news, software reviews, how-to articles, and free software downloads.

Is it that simple? Yes. Remember, if I can learn this stuff, so can you. But for those of you who want to know what's "under the hood," here it is in more detail:

The Details: In Case You Really Want to Know

The Basic Rules of Computers

1. Speed is good.

2. The higher the speed, the higher the price.

In the world of computing, speed doesn't kill. Speed is what you want: the faster the better. Got it? Everything we talk about in this chapter relates to speed. "Speed is good" is your mantra for the twenty-first century, but it comes with a price. The more speed you get the more you're going to pay.

Computers are more fun when they operate faster. My recommendation is to get the fastest computer and Internet connection you can afford. The faster your computer runs and the faster your Internet connection, the easier it's going to be to do your business on the Internet.

Computer speed is determined by the type of *processor* it uses, the amount of *RAM* (Random Access Memory) available, and the *operating system software* you're running. Think of the processor as the engine: More power equals more speed. And because it's also the brain, the more powerful it is, the better it can "think." Your computer's operating system software is your aide-de-camp. It relays your instructions to the processor, brings you what you ask for, and generally keeps the place tidy. Think of RAM as the working space in your computer.

IT'S ALL GEEK TO ME

Your computer-literate friends can talk about different kinds of processors, system software, and megabytes of RAM, but it's like having a conversation about what kind of engine is under the hood. Do you really care whether you've got a V-8 or turbocharged four cylinder? To a car nut, it matters; to the rest of us it's more like "So long as I've got enough power to have a little fun, I'm fine." Ditto computers. As a general rule, the faster the processor and the larger the amount of RAM, the faster the computer.

CAN'T I JUST UPGRADE MY MACHINE?

Although computers have components, the separate parts are really designed to operate as a whole. Upgrading your RAM won't help if your processor is too slow. Upgrading your memory won't help if the new programs can't operate with your existing RAM. By the time you upgrade all the necessary components, it's probably just easier and cheaper to buy a new machine.

The more RAM you have, the more room you have to move around in and the more you can do at the same time. Ideally, you want the newest, fastest processor, the latest version of the system software, and the most RAM you can afford to shove into your computer.

The RAM part is easy. Every computer puts that number up clearly and proudly (with a little *mb* after it to indicate "megabytes." You don't need to know what that stands for):

- 8MB is ancient. Donate it to a museum or sell it to a collector as an artifact.

- 16MB is worthless. Use it as a doorstop.

- 32MB is marginally acceptable. Two years ago it was fine, now it's barely okay.

- 64MB will get you just about anyplace you want to go in fine style.

- 128MB is cool. Three years from now it'll be marginally acceptable.

- 256MB is overkill today. Three years from now it'll probably be standard. (Are you seeing a pattern here?)

- 512MB is somewhere beyond the pale, but I've got it.

The *processor* speed is more difficult to define. The faster the processor the faster the computer (speed is good, remember?). For PC computers, processor speed is expressed in MHz (for megahertz). There's also a preliminary name or number that tells you the brand and type of processor. If the computer you're looking at has an Intel Pentium II 300MHz processor, *Intel* is the brand name, *Pentium II* is the model group, and *300MHz* indicates its speed. The bigger the MHz number, the faster it is. It's more complicated than that, but this is an online investing book, not a guide to computer shopping. In general, keep that MHz number higher than 300 (for a Pentium II or equivalent processor from AMD or others) or 350 (for a Pentium III or equivalent), and you'll be fine.

For Macintosh computers, the concept's the same, the names of the computer chips are different. The top Macintosh models, as I write this, are the G4 models; I don't think you'd want to buy anything that wasn't a G3 or G4. If you don't know much about Macs but are interested, look for someone who has one and see what he or she thinks.

Hardware, Software, What's the Difference?

> **GET A SECOND OPINION**
>
> Everyone you know who has a computer has an opinion about it. Find three of your friends who are the loudest and most opinionated. Tell them how much you want to spend on a computer, monitor, and printer. Write down their opinions. Play them off each other. Make them duke it out. Buy their consensus choice. You could do worse.

Very simple: Hardware makes the computer run. Software tells it what to do. Think of a deck of cards. The deck is the hardware, the game you choose to play is the software. You can play poker or solitaire. They're two different games with different rules, but they both use the same deck, essentially the same "hardware." Different software programs allow you to do different things with the same computer hardware, and there's software for virtually everything you'd ever want to do—Web browsing, word processing, managing your money, or playing poker and solitaire.

What You Need to Invest Online

Your Computer, Your Browser — Modem — Phone Company or Cable Connection — **ISP** Internet Service Provider — Financial Service Provider

So, why not just upgrade the software? Well, here's where the general rule gets all messed up. Newer software puts a lot of strain on older systems. Newer software does more, so it needs more room, more RAM, and more speed. An older machine with less RAM runs better with older software. Also, you've got compatibility problems associated with both the older computer and older software. As a rule, newer always seems faster and easier—for both hardware and software.

Making the Connection

That's it on the guts of the machine. Now you've got to get from your computer (or television set-top box or personal digital assistant or souped-up cell phone or whatever Web-enabled device you're using) to the Internet, and the most popular way to get there is with a *modem*.

The modem is a device inside (or attached to) the computer that connects you to the Internet through your phone line. Again, faster is better. Virtually all new computers come with a modem and all modems have a number. This number has a *k* or *kb* after it (for kilobits per second—if you don't already know, don't ask) and is the maximum speed that data can be transmitted to your computer.

- 2,400 (2.4k), 4,800 (4.8k), and 9,600 (9.6k) modems are dinosaurs that should be put in museums. Six years ago these were state of the art. Wow.

- A 14.4k modem isn't really very useful these days, other than for e-mail or with older machines. Otherwise, you'll spend your life online waiting for information to get *downloaded* (sent to your computer).

- A 28.8k modem was leading-edge a couple of years ago. You can live with it, but you won't like it. It's like doing 50 on the Interstate—it's legal, but sluggish.

- 56.6k V.90 is today's standard. Most of us can navigate the information superhighway perfectly well with one of these.

For now.

Those are the basic, off-the-shelf modems. They're also the modems of the last century. Telephone, cable, satellite, and hybrid companies are jockeying to deliver high-capacity digital services to your doorstep, and pretty soon we'll all have the following choices (which some lucky souls already enjoy) at an affordable price:

Cable. See that fat wire that goes into the back of your TV? Imagine if it could also carry data. That's what you get if your local cable operator offers cable Internet access. The speed is dazzling—about 25 times faster than a modem dial-up connection. Web pages load almost instantaneously. But there's one drawback: The cable is a shared line. The more people who go online at the same time, the slower the data flows over the lines. Despite that, for the price, it's still king of the home options. After the installation charge and the cost of a cable modem, you can expect to pay about $30 to $50 a month—generally on top of your current cable fees. Availability is limited, but growing. Call your local cable company for more information.

DSL. Digital Subscriber Line (sometimes ADSL for Asynchronous Digital Subscriber Line) is offered by local phone companies and other providers at more and more locations. DSL transmits highly compressed digital data over a portion of the phone line without interrupting your voice service. With one phone line, you can simultaneously send and receive phone calls while you're sending and receiving data online. The download speed is impressive (similar to a cable connection), but it varies based on your distance from the phone company's switching equipment. Expect to pay about $30 to $50 a month over and above your regular phone charges—on top of the installation and

> **MICK AND KEITH. DONNY AND MARIE. MODEM AND PROCESSOR.**
> Make sure you match the modem to the processor. You don't put a big V-8 in a car that can't handle that kind of power. Same with modems and processors. Although most computers can handle up to 56.6K perfectly well, when you get into the newer high-speed choices, the power of your processor becomes crucial. Don't waste your money on a cable modem if all you've got is a 133Mhz processor. No matter how fast the information comes into your computer, the processor won't be able to open it up and display it very quickly.

equipment charges for a special modem. Again, availability is limited but growing. Call your local phone company or DSL provider for more information. With both cable and DSL, when your computer is on, you're automatically connected to the Internet.

ISDN. Integrated Service Digital Network is a technological end-run around the limitations of your phone system's nineteenth-century copper wires. ISDN allows more data to flow through your phone lines at slightly higher speeds than a 56.6k modem—from 64k up to 128k. It's available in a lot of areas where other new modes may not be available or cost-effective. For more information, call your local phone company.

Satellite. If you're telecommuting from Tahiti or phone and cable companies in your neighborhood are a long way from providing new digital services, satellite data is one way to go. Compared with a 56.6k modem, satellite is currently about seven times faster—up to 400k. The disadvantage is that satellite is a one-way street. You need a satellite dish on your roof, but it can only receive, not send, so you also need to be connected to the satellite service provider by phone line in order to send outgoing e-mail. Price? Besides the cost of the satellite dish and installation, it's in the $30 to $120 a month range.

OBEY THE COMPANY RULES

Most employers have strict Internet access rules and are legally allowed to monitor and control employee usage. Although some personal usage is generally acceptable, no company is required to let you use their computers for your own purposes—and in some instances, it can be grounds for immediate dismissal. Please check your company's Internet policy, and if in doubt, do your surfing on your own computer and your own time.

T-1 Lines. This is what most businesses have, which is why all your friends stay late at work or come in early—to surf the Net on the company line. These high-capacity data lines connect to the Internet at almost instantaneous speeds. For about $500 a month, you can have a dedicated high-speed line in your house, home office, or business, with no sharing and no one-way streets. It could be the status symbol of the new century.

T-3 lines. Only very big businesses have these, and they're very expensive. The way things are going, though, they'll probably be available for home use eventually. So, if you really want to impress your techno-savvy friends and your pockets are very deep, go for it.

Those are your choices—for now! In 1965, Gordon Moore, a co-founder of Intel, predicted that the computing power of microprocessors would double every 18 months. It became known as "Moore's Law." A similar phenomenon seems to apply to the computer world as a whole. Every 18 months or so we witness a quantum leap in the capabilities of just about any device you can think of. The only thing that doesn't double every 18 months is price. In fact, for a given amount of computing power, prices decline sharply over time. New devices are coming out all the time, so don't hold me to anything in this section. Just keep in mind the two key pieces of information:

1. Speed is good.
2. The higher the speed, the higher the price.

> **CHRISTOS' COROLLARY**
>
> Every 18 months, the computing power of microprocessors doubles—and the value of your old computer is cut in half. If your instincts are to treat your computer like your stereo system—a long-term purchase with an occasional upgrade—your instincts are wrong. A three-year-old computer is a very large paperweight. And although it may pain you to think about donating your three-year-old computer to a school or charity, the upside is that for the same $1,200 you paid three years ago, today you'll get four times as much computer.

CHAPTER 3

Get Your Modem Running

" All the information I need is on the Web. **"**

J.W., Company President

Choosing an Internet Service Provider

America Online, Earthlink, Microsoft Network, Prodigy, WebTV, AT&T@Home: They're all Internet Service Providers (or "I-S-Ps" as we say). There are over 8,000 to choose from. You need one.

ISPs are like your phone company to the Internet, and they come in all sizes and flavors: local, regional, national, and international; open-access, limited-access, filtered, family friendly. Some ISPs just get you onto the Internet and leave you alone. Others, including most of the major national ones, offer vast amounts of content just for their subscribers—a sort of Internet within the Internet.

If you just bought a new computer, you probably have the software for two or three different ISP choices already installed, just waiting for you to activate them. Different computer manufacturers offer different choices, but you'll usually find the major ISPs preloaded: America Online (AOL), Prodigy Internet, Microsoft Network (MSN), Earthlink, Dell Online, AT&T, and so forth. If you got one of the super-fast cable or DSL hookups we discussed earlier, an ISP was probably part of the package—so you can skip this section.

How does Internet service work? Once you've got an ISP, you open their software or click their icon and your computer modem "dials up" the ISP over a regular phone line using a local phone number. The ISP serves as your gateway or **portal**, connecting you to the Internet through their computers.

What does it cost? Currently, $9.95 to $19.95 per month is the standard price range for unlimited (24-hour-a-day, seven-day-a-week) access, but like everything else in the digital universe, prices are coming down. A number of ISPs now promote "free" service, but you have to wade through a large number of advertisements and allow them to monitor your activity. Most services offer unlimited access for a fixed price, which means you can log on and stay on for as long as you want. Some services offer a low basic price, but then charge an hourly fee if you use more than a certain number of hours. Some ISPs offer discounts if you pay for a whole year (or two) at once. Some computer hardware manufacturers offer a $300 or $400 computer rebate if you sign up for their Internet service for a certain number of months. Start-up ISPs often offer free service to attract new subscribers and build their base. It's a good deal if their service is good, access is easy, and their lines are never busy. Internet service is one of the most competitive arenas in the computer world—so carefully review each offer.

Bottom line? You should be able to find something within your budget. It's smart to comparison shop. You could ask your local computer store for information on local and regional ISPs. Some of the major providers offer free trials. You can see if you like them, and if not use your free trial period to shop around online for another ISP, for example, check out *www.thelist.com*, a Web site that lists every known ISP. Check what's available in your area, ask your friends which ISPs they use and why they like them,

portal
A large Web site that offers lots of free information and is used as a launch pad for activities on the Web.

or check out the ISP evaluations in computer and consumer magazines.

Besides price and ease-of-use, consider three more factors when choosing an ISP.

1. How busy are their lines? No matter how fast your connection to an ISP is, you might be stuck because their actual Internet connection is all clogged up, or your connection to them is jammed with 4,000 other people living in the same neighborhood. So, one question to ask is how much traffic is on a particular ISP and how they handle that traffic.

2. How many members do they allow per account? Is your membership a single-person or family membership? Some ISPs allow only one user (and one e-mail address) per account. Others allow up to five or six.

3. How accessible are they from around the globe? If your PC isn't mobile, this is not likely to be an issue for you. If, however, you travel with a laptop, you should find out the range of geographical toll-free access points the ISP supports.

JUST BROWSING

The package you receive from your Internet Service Provider will most likely include a Web browser. You may even be given several options from which to choose. The browser controls how information from the World Wide Web is displayed on your computer screen. The two major brands are Microsoft Internet Explorer and Netscape Communicator. Both are very good and both can be downloaded free from the Internet.

Getting Online

Once you've decided which ISP you want to use, just sign up to activate your account. If you go with one of the ISPs preloaded on your computer, pick the one you want, double-click the icon, and the software will walk you through the sign-up process. If you choose a local ISP instead, you might be able to sign up over the phone. Either way, they're going to want some billing information. In general, they deduct your monthly service charges directly from the credit card you authorize. If the service is through the phone or cable company, they may add it to your regular phone or cable bill.

When you double-click the icon for your ISP using the software they provided, you'll be taken through a step-by-step process that automatically connects your computer to them through your phone line. (Hopefully, one of the steps in setting up your computer and modem was to connect the computer's modem to a phone outlet with a standard phone jack.) Note: If you have only one phone line in your house, you won't be able to make or receive phone calls while you're online (unless you use DSL or a cable service). The first time you're connected, they'll ask you to fill out an application online and choose a unique *user name* and password.

That user name plus the name of the ISP provider is the basis for your *e-mail address*. This is what you give all your friends and family and what lets you send and receive e-mail to anyone else who has an e-mail address.

Once you've signed up and selected your name, for the price of a local call plus your monthly fee, you're a Netizen!

Welcome!

Here you are on the threshold to a new universe. How do you feel? Any different? You should. The simple journey you just took has brought you into the age of individual empowerment. Savor this moment because it's one of the most important in the history of technological development and you are lucky enough to experience it. Our kids will inhabit and control a world that you and I can only dream of: a world with a universe of information and technology at their fingertips. The Web page you're looking at on your computer screen is the first faint flickering of this new world.

So much for the basic stuff. Let's go somewhere.

> **DEAR BJQ4563MB2@.com**
>
> Which ISP you sign up with determines the look of your e-mail address. So, if you join America Online (AOL), your e-mail address will end with @aol.com. What goes before the @ sign is your unique identifier and you get to choose it. The bigger the ISP, the more likely it is that a simple user name (like your first name) or a clever nickname will be taken. Other ISPs limit the number of characters you can use before the @ symbol. It might not be a big deal to you, but if it is, you may have to shop around for an ISP that will let you use the address you want.

Getting Where You Want to Go

Getting places on the Internet is like getting into a taxi in a strange city. You hop in, tell the driver the address you want to go to, and trust he'll get you there as quickly as possible. If you don't know the address, you tell the cabby approximately what you're looking for and hope you've given him enough information ("the symphony," "that all-night club") so he knows what you're talking about.

The difference? On the Internet, you don't say the address (at least not yet, though it's sure to come), you type it.

Most Internet addresses begin *http://www* (some replace the www with a different prefix). You don't need to know what this means. Think of it as the area code you dial when making a long distance call.

Want to go to E★TRADE? (Just a suggestion.) Launch your Web browser and type our Internet address in the Address box: *www.etrade.com*. Press Enter on your keyboard or click the Go button with your mouse and you're there!

OH COM ALL YE FAITHFUL

Why the .com after our address? It's the Internet protocol for commercial. Every U.S.-based site on the Internet has some suffix that defines what it is: .org is for public organizations such as a library or nonprofit charity, .gov is for government, .edu is for schools. The rest of the world uses a country code as a suffix. So. if you want to go to, say, the BBC (which has a really neat Web site), you would type *www.bbc.co.uk* (for company and United Kingdom), and just like that, you're accessing England.

Shortcuts on the Information Superhighway

"Sounds great, Christos," you might be saying. "But there are millions of Web sites. How do I find or even remember all those addresses?"

You ask great questions.

The Internet has attracted a lot of clever and inventive people, and they have developed any number of clever and inventive ways to help you find your way to where you want to go.

Intuitive addresses. Most companies on the Internet choose a simple address you can remember. That's why our site is *etrade.com* and not *theinnovatorinonlinepersonalfinancialservices.com*. If you're looking for a specific company online

and don't know its Internet address, first try typing its name followed by *.com*.

"Smart" browsers. Newer Internet browsers are programmed to "guess" what you're looking for. So, instead of typing *www.etrade.com*, you can just type *etrade* and the browser will figure out where you want to go and take you there.

Favorite Places. All Internet browsers have a feature that "remembers" (*bookmarks*) sites you've been to so that you can return there with the click of a mouse. If you're at a site you want to remember, look for the menu item on your browser screen that says "Favorite Places" or "Bookmarks" or "My Favorites" or something similar , then add that site to your list of favorites. The longer you're on the Net, the longer your list of bookmarks will grow.

Linked pages. On the Internet, a *hyperlink* is a connection to another Web address. Click an icon, symbol, or under-lined word or words, and you'll be whisked from the address you're at to another one on the Internet. If it's not where you want to be, click the Back button on your browser and you'll go back to the Web page you just left. Some Web sites do nothing but list links to other Web sites. (If you find a site like this that covers a topic you're interested in, be sure to bookmark it.)

Search engines. If you know what topic you're interested in but don't know the Web address, you can go to specialized sites

> **I'VE GOT THE BOOKMARK, NOW WHERE'S THE BOOK?**
> Some dynamic Web sites, including E∗TRADE, change their Internet sites on a regular basis to ensure the best possible service to their customers. This can confuse the "bookmarking" features in many browsers, especially on AOL. So, as far as reaching E∗TRADE goes, just use *www.etrade.com*. Bookmarks work fine for more static Web sites however.

on the Internet known as search engines. Web sites such as Yahoo!, AskJeeves, and AltaVista search through literally millions of Web pages in a fraction of a second to find the information you're looking for.

Creating Your Start Page

One of my favorite Internet shortcuts is creating your own default Internet portal or start page. Once you set this up, every time you log onto the Internet, you'll automatically go to the Web page that *you've* decided is the most important one of all the millions of Web pages out there.

It's pretty simple to do. Every Web browser has an online help section that will walk you through the process of setting up your own personal start page. You can make any site on the Internet your start page, and you can change it any time you want.

An example? Say you decide that the first thing you want to do when you get on the Web is to monitor your financial life. (This will get you in the habit of keeping tabs on your financial information on a regular basis.)

If you choose E*TRADE as your start page, the next time you log onto your ISP and launch your browser, the first thing you see will be the E*TRADE home page.

I'll be using portions of the E*TRADE Web site to illustrate various points in the chapters that follow, so why don't you make E*TRADE your "home" page while you're reading this book? It'll be easier for you to check things out and follow along. When you've finished this book, you can change your home page to anything you want. Fair enough?

C'MON TO OUR HOUSE!

If you have one of the big commercial ISPs, there are other ways of reaching E*TRADE.

America Online: Type ETRADE in the box marked Keyword on your screen, click Go, and you'll get to us.

Prodigy Internet: Select the Business and Finance channel on your screen, choose Internet Investor, go to the Online Trading area, and click E*TRADE.

Microsoft Investor: Go to *www.investor.com*. On the home page, select "Open an Account and Trade Online," then select E*TRADE.

WebTV: Select the Options button on your remote control or keyboard. Select Go. Type etrade after the http:// prefix and press Enter.

CHAPTER 4

Make It A
Good One

Choosing a Financial Service Provider

Why do you do business with a bank? Because this is my book, I get to guess: for checking and savings. You can put your paycheck into a checking account and then write checks to pay your bills. You can transfer money to and from your savings account. You can apply for a loan or get a credit card. It's a 300-year-old system that's a lot safer and more efficient than your mattress.

It's time you joined the revolution.

A good online financial service provider should give you access to a broad range of investment alternatives and all the online resources and research information you'll probably ever need to manage your money. From free checking to credit cards, mortgages, investments, financial planning, retirement—almost anything you can do that affects your financial future—you can do with an account at a good online financial service provider.

E✳TRADE. Charles Schwab. DLJdirect. Fidelity. Ameritrade. TD Waterhouse. We're all online financial service providers. You need one.

At this point you probably think I'm going to tell you to go directly to *www.etrade.com* and sign up for an account with E*TRADE. Even though I am very, very proud of what we have accomplished, I'm not going to do that.

The whole point of this book is to empower you. The worst thing you can do when managing your own money is to blindly follow someone else's advice—no matter whose it is. If I thought that was a good idea, I wouldn't have bothered to write this book.

Managing your own money online is a way of taking control of your actions, your research, your information, your decisions, and your own account. It's not a form of gambling. *Making financial decisions without knowing what you're doing **is** a form of gambling.*

A SPECIAL NOTE ABOUT ONLINE SECURITY AND ACCESS

The Internet is a complex global village. It is as safe and secure as any business venue—technology based or not. At E*TRADE, we have invested a huge amount of money and resources to ensure that our site is as secure and tamper-proof as possible—and we will continue to dedicate significant resources to always stay one step ahead. In addition to a commitment to security, be sure your online financial service provider offers multiple modes of access.

At E*TRADE, we offer our customers a number of alternative channels of access, including full account and trading capabilities through the telephone. TELE*MASTER, our touch-tone and voice recognition phone system, provides an alternative connection to market data, account information and transaction capabilities. In addition, our customers can call or email our in-house customer service representatives 24 hours a day, seven days a week, 366 days a year.

Instead of telling you what to do, I'm going to give you some guidelines to help you select the best possible financial service provider, and then set you loose on the Internet to make the right decision—*for yourself.*

So, how do you evaluate and choose a good financial service provider? Start with what I call "the six Ss": security, speed, simplicity, service, sharing, and scalability. The best financial service providers do all of these very well. That's why we've made them the backbone of E*TRADE's service.

1. Security. Are your transactions secure? Is your money safe? These are real issues you should consider when choosing a financial service provider. Insurance coverage is another important consideration. How much insurance does the company carry to safeguard customer accounts from things such as theft, embezzlement, malfeasance, and other unpleasantness? All legitimate

broker/dealers are required by NASDR to carry a minimum of $500,000 in insurance to protect the assets in
each customer account from such losses. This coverage is
purchased by member brokers through the Security
Investor Protection Corporation (SIPC). If your financial
service provider also offers traditional banking services, it
must be insured by the FDIC—the same federal insurance
that brick-and-mortar banks carry. Many online financial
service providers carry other insurance as well. E*TRADE
provides an additional $99.5 million in coverage on each
customer account through the National Union Fire
Insurance Company of Pittsburgh, PA. So, you're insured
up to a million in cash and $99,500,000 in securities when
you invest with us. Remember: All this insurance is to
protect you from things over which you, the customer, have
no control. No one can guarantee that your investments
will always make money, and no insurance policy will
repay you if your investments lose money. In addition to
the SIPC, another logo you should look for is the CPA
WebTrust seal, which assures you that your privacy is
protected and your transactions are as safe and secure as
those conducted in person.

2. Speed. In the financial markets, time can mean everything. How quickly will they handle your order and let you
know it's been executed? Not every provider executes or
arranges for the execution of orders equally fast, because
sometimes the **information superhighway** suffers traffic
jams. Orders received by financial service providers need
to be routed to marketplaces for execution which may also
suffer traffic jams during high volume periods. This is a
significant issue because the Internet and the financial
markets are high-volume environments. All online financial
service providers depend on the national communications
network of ISPs to connect with customers. The more on
and off ramps to this electronic highway your online
provider has, the better your access. This can be particularly
critical (especially if you're an active investor) during

In the Web We
Trust

TRUST·e

Look for these
certifications. The
CPA (Certified Public
Accountants) WebTrust
seal indicates the
site has passed an
independent CPA
audit of safety and
security. The TRUSTe
privacy program certi-
fication ensures that
your personal informa-
tion is kept private.
E*TRADE was the
first to receive both
certifications.

**information
superhighway**
Another term for
the Internet.

trading periods when the stock market is moving rapidly. In situations when you think it's critical to place a buy or sell order, you don't want a site that crashes trying to keep up with the heavy two-way traffic flow. And although no system is delay-free, a fully redundant routing system of multiple connections helps to guard against this. E*TRADE, for example, has connections to seven different ISPs to ensure you'll have access to your account and your money.

3. Simplicity. How easy is it to use? When you go to the Web site of any financial service provider, what do you see? How readable is their home page? How easy is it to get from there to any other place on the site? Try each financial service provider you're considering. The easier it is to navigate through the site, the easier it's going to be to manage your money and find the information you want.

4. Service. There comes a time when you're going to reach for the phone. You'll have a moment of doubt or need tech support or want to ask service questions or experience uncertainty. Who's gonna be there when you call? Try it. Call every financial service provider you're considering and see how long it takes to get a human being on the line. Are they available 24 hours a day, seven days a week, 365 days a year (366 in leap years)? Do you always get someone on the phone or do you get routed through one of those endless telephone "trees" we've all come to dread? If you're put on hold, do you like their choice in music? And how long do you have to listen to it? There's no such thing as too much service.

5. Sharing. A good financial service provider will be generous in sharing its information with you and letting you share your information with others. This is the kind of immediate, one-to-one communication the Internet is so

---

THE LARGE PRINT GIVETH AND THE SMALL PRINT TAKETH AWAY.

Sometimes the fees charged by a financial service provider look almost too good to be true. Maybe they are. Be sure to check for extra fees and costs such as minimum balances. The Internet has transformed the world, but some things never change—we still say "Caveat Emptor" (Let the buyer beware) in Latin almost 2,000 years after the Roman Empire fell.

good at creating. Does the financial service provider you're considering offer the widest possible access to real-time market information? Do they provide tutorials and simulations that allow you to learn more about financial planning and test out your investment strategies before you risk your hard-earned money? Do they provide you with just their opinion, or do they give you access to a broad range of commentary and ready access to content from other sites with independent market coverage? Even more important, does the financial service provider you're considering facilitate the creation of community among its customers, allowing you to communicate directly with other investors to share your successes and setbacks? At E*TRADE we have public forums for both real-time chat and discussion groups, where more than a quarter of a million investors communicate with each other about virtually any topic, ask questions, and assist each other in their mutual goal of becoming more informed investors.

> **What I look for in an online broker is how well they handle high volume days and their system capacity.**
>
> A.C., Business Manager

6. Scalability. Will they love you when you're small? Will you love them when you're big? Pick a financial service provider you can grow and change with. Consider not only what your needs are today, but what they may become down the road. Just want to buy some Certificates of Deposit today? Fine. But what happens if you become an active investor? Will the online service you choose be able to handle your increased volume with equal efficiency, as well as provide you with the different tools you'll need to become a more active trader? And what about diversification? Today, perhaps you're only into stocks. But if you decide to move into mutual funds next year, what will you do with a stocks-only online broker? Will you be able to shop for mutual funds with them? Will they have the information and selection you need? Will they have the tools to help you identify funds based on your investing criteria?

The Seventh "S"

There's one more "S" you'll probably consider when select-ing an online financial service provider, but I rank it lower than the other six: savings. Some financial service providers charge less for certain transactions than others do. They all have different rate structures, but compared with what it used to cost to have someone else managing your money or running your account, every online financial service provider can save you money. The real savings come from the information and services they offer and the structure they provide to access that information.

Finding the financial service provider that's right for you will take a little time and effort. Do it. Not only will you be sure, on a deep and fundamental level, that you made the right decision, but you'll have developed research and analysis skills that will come in handy down the road.

Accounts and Access

As of 3/00		E·TRADE	Schwab	Ameritrade	Merrill Lynch
Minimum Balance*		$1,000	$5,000	$2,000	$20,000
Individual Accounts		Yes	Yes	Yes	Yes
Joint Accounts		Yes	Yes	Yes	Yes
Business Accounts		Yes	Yes	Yes	Yes
Custodial Accounts		Yes	Yes	Yes	Yes
Retirement Accounts					
IRA Accounts		Yes	Yes	Yes	Yes
Roth IRA Accounts		Yes	Yes	Yes	Yes
SEP Accounts		Yes	Yes	Yes	Yes
Investing Accounts					
Cash Accounts	(minimum)	$1,000	$5,000	$2,000	$20,000
Margin Accounts	(minimum)	$2,000	$10,000	$2,000	$20,000
Access to Account Information					
Online Access		Yes	Yes	Yes	Yes
Touch-tone Phone		Yes	Yes	Yes	Yes
Speech Recognition		Yes	Limited	No	Yes
24-hour Customer Service Rep Support		Yes	Yes	Yes	Yes
Wireless Device Access		Yes	Yes	Yes	No

*Special promotions may change requirements.

This information is subject to change without notice and does not represent a complete listing of services offered by the companies listed above or of all online financial service providers.

CHAPTER 5

Open Your Account Today

Opening an Online Account

How do you open an online account? Fill out and submit an account application form, get approved, fund your account instantly, and begin investing and managing your funds online.

It's that simple. If you don't believe me, add another "S" to your search criteria: sign-up simplicity. I think you'll find most financial service providers have made the sign-up process painless. The difference is in the details. Your job is to make sure the information you provide is accurate and complete to allow for timely review and approval.

Types of Online Accounts

Most online financial service providers offer the basic investing accounts discussed here—and some offer more. You have a lot of choices—and some questions to ask yourself. Who owns the assets in the account? How do you want those assets to be used? What happens to those assets if you die? There are legal and tax ramifications to those choices and they vary from state to state. If you're not sure which one to choose, it's smart to consult an attorney or tax advisor before opening your account.

Individual Accounts. Assets held in an individual account are owned and may be used by only one person: you.

Joint Accounts. Joint accounts are owned and may be used (with mutual consent) by two or more people—for example, you and your spouse. Joint accounts can be set up in different ways, depending on what you want to have happen should one of you die:

- **Joint Right of Survivorship.** If one of the owners dies, total interest and control of his or her share of the assets passes immediately to the survivor. If something happens to you, the other owner of the account would assume title to everything in the account without any inconvenient legal hassles.

- **Joint Tenants-in-Common.** You can share this type of account among multiple account owners (two or more). And the percentage of ownership can vary (not necessarily 50/50). If one of the owners dies, interest and control of that person's share of the assets passes to his or her estate. If something were to happen to you, your share of the account would pass to the person (or persons) you specified in your will; this can tie up the assets in an account until your will is settled—or longer if you don't have a will.

- **Community Property.** An account owned by a couple living in a state that recognizes community property. You may want to consult with an attorney for a complete description of the legal implications associated with this type of account.

Custodial Accounts. Want to give your niece some shares of stock and teach her the ins and outs of managing her finances right from the start? Good for you! When you open an account for a minor, it has to be as a custodial account, because minors are prohibited from owning securities directly. Custodial accounts are opened under the rules regarding the Uniform Gifts to Minors Act (known as UGMA) or Uniform Transfers to Minors Act (UTMA). You get to choose which one, and the rules differ from state to state. Because there are tax consequences to either, check with a tax professional as to which would be best for you. When the child turns 18, he or she will assume full title and control of the account.

Business Accounts. These are a smart idea if you want to maximize the value of your company's accounts receivables and accounts payables. There are a number of different types of business accounts.

- **Corporate.** This type of account is registered to a business that is incorporated and is an asset of that business.

- **Sole Proprietorship.** This is an account registered to a business with a single owner who is, in effect, the business and therefore holds all of the assets in the account. If that person dies, the assets in the account pass to his or her estate.

- **Partnerships.** This account can be used with mutual consent by two or more owners of the business in whose name the account is registered. If the partnership dissolves or one of the partners dies, the account's assets are disbursed or pass to the survivor according to the terms of the partnership.

Investment Club Accounts. This isn't a business, but an account used by a group of people for mutual investing. These have become very popular in recent years thanks to some best-selling books about successful clubs. Even though an investment club can have many members, one or two people act as the agent(s) for the entire club when making investments for the account.

Trust and Estate Accounts. Establishing accounts for your children can be a smart way to lower your taxes and teach them the value of saving. Unfortunately, giving your children control of that money can be a not-so-smart way for them to show you the value of the new sports car they bought. Establishing a trust or estate account can give you the tax benefits—while keeping some measure of control over the money.

Online Retirement Accounts

Every once in a while, Congress gets it right. Or if they don't then they sometimes try again, which probably explains why there are so many different types of retirement accounts. I can't explain why Congress created so many variations, but I can introduce you to the available options. You should consult a tax advisor (again!) to discuss what works best for you. When our elected representatives in Washington, D.C. created the Individual Retirement Account (IRA), they hit a home run. With IRAs, there's no excuse not to be saving for retirement.

If you don't have an IRA, get one. If you don't understand why you should have one, get one anyway. You'll understand soon enough. If you're 20-something, great! You've got plenty of time to get rich. If you're 50-something and haven't saved a nickel, it's still not too late. Honest.

All retirement accounts have several things in common:

- They're designed to get you to save money.
- They provide you with some tax relief. Subject to income limits, which I'll discuss shortly, the money you contribute to a retirement account may be tax-deductible and the money the account earns is tax-deferred—meaning you don't have to pay taxes on the money until you start withdrawing it from the account after a certain age.
- You can choose among several types of securities to invest in.

Congress quickly realized the original IRA was a winner and they've been adding new variations over the years. Today, you have a fairly wide range of different retirement accounts to choose from:

Traditional IRAs. These are America's most popular retirement plans—with almost $2 trillion invested in them to date. You can contribute up to $2,000 of earned income a year ($4,000 if you're married). Contributions are tax-deductible unless you're enrolled in a qualified employer-sponsored retirement plan such as a 401(k) and/or your Adjusted Gross Income (AGI) is higher than $25,000 ($40,000 if you're married). The money these accounts earn is tax-deferred until you start making withdrawals. In most cases, age 59½ is the earliest you can start withdrawing without paying a 10 percent penalty to the IRS. And age 70½ is the longest you can leave your money untouched without being hit with a stiff tax on the minimum distribution you haven't taken.

Rollover IRAs. If you change employers or retire, you may receive a lump sum payment from your company. This money is fair game for the IRS—Uncle Sam will want his share unless you use a Rollover IRA. If you put the money you receive into an IRA account (roll it over) within 60 days, you avoid the penalties. Once you've done that, if you're not retired you can keep contributing to it like a regular IRA (and/or combine it with a regular IRA) or move the assets to your new employer's plan, whichever you prefer.

Simplified Employee Pension Plans (SEP-IRAs). This is a simple way for employers to provide a retirement benefit for employees. "But I'm self-employed," you say. Exactly. The "employee" whose retirement you can contribute to is you. And here's the good news: You can contribute either $30,000 or up to 15 percent of the employee's salary— whichever is less. There is a cap on the salary at $160,000 —which means you can contribute up to $24,000 a year.

The money goes in tax-free and isn't taxed until you begin withdrawing it. But once the money is in the account, the owner of the account (you) decides how to invest it.

Savings Incentive Match Plan for Employees (SIMPLE IRAs). This salary reduction plan is designed for companies with fewer than 100 employees. Participants can contribute up to $6,000 annually, tax-deferred; employers are required to make a matching contribution to each plan, and they get a tax deduction for their match.

Roth IRAs. These were created by the Taxpayer Relief Act of 1997 to help investors sock as much money as they want into an IRA even if they have an employer-sponsored retirement plan. Contributions are not tax-deductible—but earnings are tax-free. You pay taxes on the money you put in, but once it's in there, whatever you earn isn't taxed. Withdrawals can be made before retirement without paying a penalty if you've held the account for at least five years and the withdrawal is used to buy a first home or to pay for your child's college education. You can contribute to a Roth IRA as long as you live, there is no maximum age requirement for starting withdrawals, and whatever money is left in your account after you die passes to your heirs tax-free.

Which one is right for you? Or which ones are right for you? A good financial service provider will provide research tools to help you make an informed decision, but here's a simple quiz that can steer you in the right direction:

How to Choose Between a Traditional IRA or Roth IRA

1. My main investment concern is tax-deferred growth.
☐ yes ☐ no

2. My main investment concern is tax-sheltered growth.
☐ yes ☐ no

3. I expect my tax bracket to drop when I retire.
☐ yes ☐ no

4. I expect my tax bracket to be the same or higher when I retire.
☐ yes ☐ no

5. I participate in a retirement plan at work.
☐ yes ☐ no

6. I may have to dip into my savings before retirement.
☐ yes ☐ no

7. My adjusted gross income is more than $100,000.
☐ yes ☐ no

8. My adjusted gross income is less than $100,000.
☐ yes ☐ no

9. I need the tax deduction for contributions.
☐ yes ☐ no

10. I want to keep funding my plan as long as I'm breathing.
☐ yes ☐ no

RESULTS: If you answered *yes* to questions 1, 3, 7, and 9, a traditional IRA may be your best bet. But a *yes* to questions 2, 4, 5, 6, 7, 8, and 10 would indicate that a Roth IRA (or converting from a traditional IRA if you have one to a Roth) may make the most financial sense. You won't, however, be able to determine your eligibility for either plan and determine which one is best for you until you actually run the numbers.

Check out the Retirement Center at E*TRADE. It provides the tools and information to help you determine which type of retirement account is right for you. E*TRADE does not currently give tax advice, but whatever type of retirement account you choose, you should be able to open it and manage the money online.

Investing Levels

You and your financial service provider must agree on how, and under what conditions, you can buy and sell securities. This arrangement is known as your investing or trading level. You have to meet certain conditions to trade in riskier types of securities (such as options) or to engage in certain strategies, or to borrow against assets in your account.

Cash. The most basic investing arrangement. You can invest only as much cash as you've got in your account to buy stocks, bonds, and mutual funds.

Margin. In addition to cash investing, you're extended a line of credit to buy certain classes of stocks or bonds using the securities themselves or assets in your accounts as collateral for the interest-bearing loan. You increase your purchasing power—but incur debt and increase your financial risk if your investment choices don't pan out.

Trading on Margin

Trading on margin is like those equity loans people sometimes take out on their houses. You can use the appraised value of certain assets to borrow money. Of course, you'll pay interest on the money you borrow—and your net account value is lowered by the amount of the loan outstanding. Instead of your house, though, you get to borrow from your financial service provider against the value of the cash and securities you've paid for in order to do more investing. So, if you're paying 9 percent interest, and your portfolio gains 15 percent a year, you're making a 6 percent profit off other people's money.

There are a lot of rules involved, and even the most basic discussion is more than I can get into here, but I want to point out some important facts. (You can also get some helpful information at the SEC's Web site at *www.sec.gov*.)

1. You can't necessarily trade everything you want on margin, and not everything in your account may be marginable. Stocks have to be trading at a certain price level (generally, over $5) to be considered eligible equity for margin and must also be deemed *marginable* by the **Fed**.

2. Margin trading is risky, when it doesn't work, it can put you into a margin call. Remember those stories about people jumping out the windows during the Crash of 1929? This is an extreme version of what happened to them—try not to let it happen to you. Margin calls aren't worth jumping out the window, but they are pretty serious.

"So, what's a margin call?"

A call in your margin account occurs when the percentage of what you owe versus what your account is worth (your **account equity**) reaches the point at which the regulations and/or the financial service provider's rules require you to deposit additional funds. Here is *a very basic* example of how this percentage is calculated.

Let's say you have an account with a market value of $5,000 and no outstanding loans. If you borrow another $5,000 and use that money to purchase an equivalent amount of stock, the market value of your account would now be $10,000 and your **equity percentage** (a very important figure to watch) would be 50 percent. This means that 50 percent of your account's market value is fully paid for and 50 percent is on margin—essentially purchased with a loan from your financial service provider.

So let's say the stock moves up, and now the market value of the account is $15,000. You still owe the $5,000 you borrowed. Your account equity, however, is now $10,000. And your equity percentage (market value divided by account equity) is 67 percent. You've made money by investing the borrowed money. Good for you!

But let's say the stock moves down, and now the market value of your account has shrunk from $10,000 to

the Fed
Short for the Federal Reserve. This is the central bank in the U.S. that oversees money supply, interest rates and credit. Their goal is to keep the U.S. economy stable.

account equity
The total amount of assets (cash and fully-owned securities) in an account minus any liabilities (amounts borrowed and still owed).

equity percentage
In a margin account, this percentage is calculated by dividing the market value of the cash and fully-owned securities by the market value of the amount owed on margin (borrowed funds).

$7,500. You still owe the $5,000 you borrowed and your equity percentage has dropped to 33 percent. Margin call time! Every provider has different margin maintenance requirements, but if your equity goes down that low, you'd either be in a margin call or awfully close to one.

Again, there are a lot of details involved with this, and I'm not going to discuss all of them here. You do need to know one thing about margin calls: You need to respond *immediately*. Why? Your financial service provider is **required by law** to bring your account back into compliance —to make sure your ratio is within regulatory guidelines. To do that, they can take action (sell securities in your account) at any time, with or without letting you know beforehand. Don't let this scare you—but don't get burned. The rules and ins and outs of margin trading are complex and can be confusing. It's not for everybody. Again, the SEC Web site has good information on margin rules (*www.sec.gov/consumer/onlitips.htm*) as well as a host of other valuable and practical information—and don't ever hesitate to ask your financial service provider any questions you may have.

"Can I trade on margin from the get-go?"

The answer to this depends on the financial service provider and the type of account you have. E*TRADE requires a minimum initial deposit of $2,000 to begin margin trading—a government regulation. You have to have at least $2,000 in marginable equity in your account before you can begin to borrow on margin. Whether a purchase may be made on margin, how much of the purchase price must be in your account at the time you place your order, and your margin account maintenance requirements (the minimum amount of equity you must have in your margin account at all times) are determined by Federal Reserve Board policy, by applicable exchange rules, and by your financial service provider.

Which investing level is right for you?

If you're new to investing, keep it simple. Start with a cash account. Get comfortable with managing your own finances online. There's plenty of time to explore other, more sophisticated (and riskier) investment strategies.

Opening Your Account—Online

We want your business. So does everyone else. We're all going to make it as easy as possible to open an account, starting with our home pages. Just click "Open an Account" (or similar term such as "Apply for an Account") and fill in the information requested depending on the type of account you want to open. Or pick up the phone to request a paper application form; all online financial service providers have toll-free numbers.

If you want to open an individual or joint account, IRA, or custodial account, you'll probably be able to complete all the necessary forms online. More complex accounts, such as corporate accounts and investment clubs, usually involve requesting a special application that will be sent to you by mail. (See "Types of Online Accounts" earlier in

---

Online Application

Step ❶ Select the type of account you wish to open: (select one)　　**? HELP**

- ● **Cash** account—requires full funds for purchases
- ○ **Margin** account—allows you to borrow against the assets in your account
- ○ **Margin** account with **options** trading

How will you provide your initial deposit? (check at least one)　　❶ **$1,000 minimum**
for cash accounts
- ☑ **FUND INSTANTLY** (transfer funds from your checking account)　　**$2,000 minimum**
for margin accounts
- ☐ **Check enclosed**
- ☐ **Transfer an account** from a brokerage, mutual fund or bank
- ☐ **Securities certificate(s)** enlosed (such as stock certificates)

< GO BACK　　**CONTINUE >**

this chapter for more information on the types of accounts you can open.)

The information you'll be asked for is much like what you'd be asked to provide if you were opening an account at your neighborhood bank—with some important differences. You'll be asked how you want to invest. Do you want a cash account, which requires you to pay cash for all purchases? Or do you want a margin account that lets you borrow against certain assets already in your account when buying stocks? Or do you want to trade options?

The type of account you choose can determine your minimum deposit. You can deposit more than the minimum, but you must deposit at least the minimum amount before you can begin investing.

At E*TRADE, for investing accounts we require a minimum deposit of $1,000 for cash accounts and $2,000 for margin accounts. (Some financial service providers require minimum deposits of as much as $20,000.) Remember what I said about scalability in the last chapter? The minimum deposit immediately tells you how friendly a financial service provider is to small or beginning accounts.

Finally, you'll either create or be assigned a user name and a password. (If you choose the same user name as the one you use for your ISP, make sure you choose a different password for security reasons.)

Some online financial service providers have made it possible to open an account online, fund it immediately (also online), and begin trading the same day. At E*TRADE we call it Real-Time Account Opening and it works like this: You tell us the name of your bank, your checking account number, and your bank's routing number (the numbers on the bottom of your check that appear just before your account number), and the amount you want to send us to fund your account. We'll move the money electronically from your bank account to E*TRADE and you'll have some of the money available instantly to start investing.

Opening Your Account by Mail

Maybe the online financial service provider you're considering doesn't open accounts immediately, or maybe you just don't like to be rushed. Every online financial service provider I know of lets you open your account by mail. At E*TRADE, just click the "Open an Account" link, and then click the "Apply by Mail" button on the account application screen and tell us which type(s) of account(s) you want to open. You'll receive a new account package from us by mail. Just follow the instructions, sign where indicated, and return the forms with your initial deposit.

Making Your Initial Deposit

Different financial service providers have different requirements when it comes to making your initial deposit. Here are the typical choices you can make—see what fits your needs:

Check. The most common way to initially fund an account is by check. At E*TRADE we accept personal checks, cashier's checks, and money orders.

Wire Transfer. You can send money electronically by wire transfer. Instruct your bank or financial institution to wire funds to the financial service provider of your choice. Here at E*TRADE, if we receive your wired funds by 6:30 P.M. eastern time, your money will be available the next day.

Online Cash Transfers. You can automatically transfer funds from a bank account on which you can write checks to your online account. Setting up a cash transfer system requires sending your financial service provider a voided check from your bank account, so it takes about a week or so before you can make your first transfer.

> **WHO SAID IT HAD TO BE "ALL OR NOTHING"?**
>
> If you're not ready to put all your money into your online account, you don't have to. It's your money, remember? Open your online account with just a portion of your assets and continue to maintain your traditional accounts and relationships. As you get more comfortable online, you can transfer out of accounts that are costing you too much or aren't really serving your investment needs.

Account Transfers. You can easily arrange to transfer an existing account (containing cash, stocks, mutual funds or bonds) from a traditional or online brokerage company, mutual fund, or bank to your new financial service provider. Just complete the appropriate Account Transfer form.

Securities Certificates. If you have actual stock certificates or other negotiable securities in your possession, you can sign them and send them in with your application. Remember, if you're sending in signed, negotiable securities, you should send them via certified or overnight mail so that you'll have a record. Note that once the certificates are put into your account, they will typically no longer exist in physical form. Instead, the securities will be registered in **street name** and held in your account.

street name
Term applied to securities held in the name of the financial service provider on behalf of the actual owner. Holding securities in street name can make it easier to complete a sales transaction.

As soon as your application form is approved and your deposit received, we'll send a customer kit to you. At E*TRADE, the kit includes your account information, password confirmation, and a customer agreement letter explaining terms, conditions, regulatory practices, benefits, commissions, and fee schedules. Your account is activated and you're ready for action.

Passwords

No matter how secure your financial service provider is, your account is only as secure as your personal password. Passwords give you (and no one else) access to your account information, and they make sure it's you (and no one else) buying and selling securities on your account. Some companies will assign you an ID and password and some (such as E*TRADE) allow you to create your own. This is what I *wouldn't* do:

- I wouldn't pick an obvious password. Most people pick their middle name, date of birth, street address, maiden name, kids' names, pets' names, or kids' dates of birth. If I came up with those, someone else could too.

- I wouldn't use the same password that I use for my ISP. If you inadvertently give that one out or someone learns it, they now have the password for your financial accounts.

- I wouldn't store my password on my computer. Many Internet browsers give you the option of saving your password on the browser so it's automatically available whenever you return to a site. Bad idea. Then anyone who logs onto your computer can log onto that account.

- I wouldn't write my password down next to the computer—even if it's taped to a piece of paper underneath your desk or in back of your drawer.

- I wouldn't write my password down in my address book (or enter it into my PDA—personal digital assistant) next to the listing for "password" or "online account."

When it comes to passwords, be creative. Be mysterious. But don't be so clever that you always forget it. How about your favorite vacation spot? The first bar that legally served you a drink? The address of the first house you lived in? The secret nickname you wish everyone in high school had called you?

At E*TRADE, you can have different passwords and user IDs for each account or use the same ID and password for all. One ID and password spares you from having to remember a lot of different passwords and enables you to link accounts together and access any one of them with a minimum number of keystrokes. Multiple passwords increase your personal level of security, but also increase the chances you might forget which password belongs to which account.

SERVICE FOR ONE

If e-commerce is teaching us anything, it's the classic rule of retailing: service, service, service. You've got the power to demand great service. With the click of a mouse you can go from anywhere in the world—to anyone in the world. If you're going to stay a loyal customer, you'd better get world-class service. It's something we all aim for and it's something you should demand.

If you *do* forget your password, don't worry.

Your account information is on file digitally (and securely)

Comparison Shop
Use this chart as
a quick reference
to compare account
features.

in your financial service provider's database. If you forget your password, every online financial service provider should have some security procedure to make sure you're the person you claim to be and then another procedure to provide you with a new password or to remind you of what your old password is. Sometimes that means they'll mail you a new password or a reminder of your old password.

A Sampler of Services

As of 3/00	E•TRADE	Schwab	Fidelity	Ameritrade	DLJdirect	TD Waterhouse
Minimum initial investment for brokerage accounts*	$1,000	$5,000	$5,000	$2,000	No minimum	$1,000
Commission to trade 800 shares of a Listed stock	$14.95**	$29.95	$25.00	$8.00	$20.00	$12.00
No-fee IRAs with no minimum balance	Yes	No	No	No	Yes	Yes
Free unlimited real-time stock quotes	Yes	Limited	No	Limited	Limited	Yes
On-site community discussion groups	Yes	Limited	No	No	No	No
Free Web and e-mail message alerts based on targets you set	Yes	Yes	Yes	Yes	Yes	Yes
Online mutual fund selection tools	Yes	Yes	Yes	Limited	Limited	Limited
Online mutual fund prospectus delivery	5,000+	Limited	Limited	No	No	No
Stock, option, and mutual fund trading using touch-tone and voice recognition	Yes	Limited	Yes	No	No	No
Free streaming Level II quotes for active traders	Yes	No	No	No	No	No
Free e-mail address	Yes	No	No	No	No	No
Online learning and self-service center	Yes	Yes	No	Yes	No	Yes
24 x 7 x 366 free customer service	Yes	Yes	Yes	Yes	Yes	Yes

*Special promotions may change requirements.
**For very active investors, commissions can be $4.95 per transaction.
This information is subject to change without notice and does not represent a complete listing of services offered by the companies listed above or of all online financial service providers.

Transferring or Closing Your Online Account

If you want to transfer to a different provider, your new financial service provider will initiate the transfer on your behalf once you've submitted an account application and transfer form. If you have securities in your account and don't want to transfer them, you have some choices: You could make a partial transfer, sell all the shares or have them issued to you in certificate form.

If for any reason you want to close an account (So soon? You just joined us.), just contact your financial service provider by phone, mail, or e-mail with your account number handy and say you want out. Some online providers will ask you why you're closing it. Not because we're nosy, but because we want to know if it's something we did. Or didn't do. Feedback helps us improve our service (and hopefully brings you back aboard).

If there are funds left in your account when you close it, your financial service provider will follow your instructions and send you a check or wire the money to you.

CHAPTER 6

Know Where You're Going

Know the Rules

There are rules.

They're not my rules. They're not Wall Street's rules, they're the basic rules of financial planning. If you don't follow them, you haven't got a chance. Follow them and you could be on your way to your first million. It's that simple.

Here are the rules of engagement:

1. Make a plan.

2. Take into account your strengths and weaknesses.

3. Review the plan often and change it as your needs and circumstances change.

Follow these rules and you'll be a lot smarter about your financial needs. You'll also be a lot smarter about a lot of things in your life, but that's just a bonus.

So, how are you planning to achieve financial independence?

- **Gen-Y'ers:** The day before you move out of your parents' house isn't the time to wonder how you'll pay the rent.

- **Gen-X'ers:** Your kids' senior year of high school isn't the time to start saving for college.

- **Baby Boomers:** The year before your retirement isn't the best time to start thinking about your Golden Years.

If any of that sounds familiar, you need a new plan. And it needs to be *your plan, not anybody else's.*

If you don't know what you want your money to do, then nothing you read about investing will have any meaning.

"I wanna be rich!" you say.

Yeah, yeah, we've all been there. Maybe you will be, but that's a dream, not a plan. Grab a pad and pen and, as we go through these fundamental financial planning tips, start outlining a realistic plan for yourself.

1. Outline Your Personal Financial Goals.

What's the difference between "having a plan" and "a financial goal"? Taking that cruise around the world, buying a house or a vintage sports car—those are dreams or plans. Your financial goal is how much money you'll need to get there—and how you'll get that money. It's one thing to say "I want to take a year off and hike the Appalachian Trail." What you *should* be saying is, "I want to be able to take a year off and hike the Appalachian Trail, *and* I'm going to need $50,000 to do it, so I better cut my overhead." Now you have the plan and the financial goal you need to make things happen. Got it? Take a few minutes and outline your current financial goals. Grab a pad and make three columns. On the left, write down every goal you have—short and long term. In the middle, write down how much money you think you'll need to get there. On

FINANCIAL INDEPENDENCE

Just what is financial independence? Is it really the lottery-inspired myth of being able to take this job and shove it? Or is it a sense of security that can serve as a foundation for all the decisions you make in life? "Can I afford to take a job that pays less but is more satisfying than the one I have now?" "Will my kids be able to choose from any college they want?" "Do I know I won't have to rely on Social Security to make ends meet at age 65?"

"Financial independence" is one of those catchy phrases that means different things to different people at different times in their lives. So, before you read any further, take a few minutes and write down your personal definition of financial independence. If it includes "take this job and shove it," well, more power to you.

the right, you're going to write down the plan you have to get there—after you read this chapter.

2. Know Your Strengths. What are you capable of doing? Tell the truth. And don't tell it to me, tell yourself. In the back, I've listed some financial planning books as reference tools that can give you more information. But what counts is what you can do. Can you put some money aside every week? Everything you do, everything you read, all your personal habits and quirks can be turned into tools that can help you take control of your finances. Do you keep on top of what's going on in your profession? You can use that knowledge to identify stocks and bonds to research. Make your strengths work for you.

3. Know Where You Stand Financially.
Start tracking what's coming in, what's going out, and where it's going. Once you know, establish a budget so you can treat investing as a regular, planned expense. If you're a person who thinks that way, you've probably done this already. If you aren't, then what's the point? Well, just try it for one day. Take a notepad and write down all your expenses—even the smallest items. Cash, charges, track it all. If you can, do it for a couple of days or even a week. It can start to make you conscious of where your money goes.

4. Reduce Debt. Take out your high-interest credit cards. Cut 'em up. Pay cash. Reduce the amount of money you're spending each month on interest payments. Seems pretty elementary, doesn't it? So, how come America's personal debt is at an all-time high? As I'm writing this, it's in the neighborhood of $1.4 *trillion* and growing at an annual rate of 3.75 percent. (Source: Federal Reserve; I found it on the Internet.) If we all know the right thing to do, how come we're not doing it? Human nature. Don't feel bad, you're not alone. But that's no excuse. Be one of the courageous few. Cut up those cards and get out of debt.

BUDDY, CAN YOU SPARE A DIME?
I have a friend who never uses his change. All day long, he pays for things with bills and sticks the change in his pocket. At the end of the day, he tosses all the change into a pot. Every three months, he takes the pot to the bank and invests the cash. His PCA (pocket change account) already has more than $23,000 in it for his kids' college expenses—and he's never "saved" a dime.

5. Invest Small, Steady Amounts Regularly. Can you spare $1,300 a year? How about $25 a week? It's the same amount. But one looks easier than the other. Investing small amounts on a regular basis is a smart investment strategy for most people. It promotes savings and discipline and is a lot easier on your nerves. The opposite "strategy" (if you can call it that) is the old "buy low, sell high" trick: The idea is you invest once, when the market or the stock is at its lowest, and then sell once when the market or stock is at its highest. Trouble is, very few seem to get it right. With the slow-but-steady strategy, you are constantly buying (investing) and selling only when it makes sense—for you and your financial goals.

6. Asset Allocation, or Don't Put All Your Eggs in One Basket. Once you understand what you want your money to do for you, it's tempting to pick one stock or one bond or one mutual fund and put all your money there. Smart investors diversify. They mix different types of securities (stocks, bonds, and mutual funds) and carefully balance how much of each they own. Keep this general rule in mind—don't worry about the details. Later in this book we'll talk about what those different kinds of securities are and how they affect each other, so you'll have a better idea of how to "mix and match" to manage your risk. Just keep diversification in mind as a good rule of thumb.

7. Ask Questions. This is a good financial strategy and a good life strategy. The more you ask, the more you'll learn. The more you learn, the more you'll know. The more you know, the better the chance that you'll do the right thing. Later on, we'll talk about the questions to ask—and where to look for the answers.

AN ABOVE-AVERAGE INVESTMENT PLAN

Investing small, regular amounts is sometimes called dollar cost averaging. It allows you to invest amounts that are comfortable for you and, because your total investment is spread out over months or years, it provides some protection from swings in the market. In the Mutual Funds section you'll find a detailed explanation of this investment technique.

8. Plan for the Long Haul. Investments go up in value. Investments go down in value. If the smallest downward movement prompts you to sell in a panic, you'll lose the benefit of investing. If even large downward movements prompt you to sell in a panic, you could lose the benefit of investing. You're in this for the long haul. Taking the long view generally produces the greatest possible return.

9. Keep Uncle Sam in Mind. In America, there are three great ways and one bad way to reduce your taxes. Here are the good ways:

1. Buy a house. The mortgage interest is tax-deductible.

2. Establish a retirement savings plan (see my next point).

3. Keep stocks long term. Uncle Sam taxes money earned by investment at a lower rate than most other forms of earnings. If you keep your stocks for more than a year, Uncle Sam considers them long-term capital gains and taxes your profits at either your current tax rate or 20 percent, whichever is *lower*.

What's the bad way to pay less taxes? Earn less money. You don't want to go that way.

HOT TIPS CAN EARN OR BURN

At some point in your financial future, someone will come to you with a "sure thing." As they say in the movies, it'll be someone you trust the most, someone you'd never dream could steer you wrong. No matter how much you want to go along, be very, very careful of the proverbial sure thing. Do your homework. It could be the Apollo moon shot or the Titanic.

Warning: Trading on non-public information, whether you're an insider or an outsider, can get you into a lot of trouble. You need to understand the difference. For more information, go to *www.sec.gov.*

10. Establish A Retirement Savings Plan. If you don't already have one, start one. If you already have one, keep adding to it. It lowers your taxable income today and paves the way for a financially secure tomorrow. This is where I part ways with the financial planning books. They talk about "personal financial goals" as being different from "saving for retirement." I don't. I think if you take care of the most important thing first—your financial future—all the rest will get solved along the way. Or at least you'll be able to sort out what the best choices are.

Doubling Your Money and The Rule of 72

Why invest? Why take control of your own money? Should you look at stocks or bonds? You've made a plan and outlined your goals, but how do you start?

No two people have the same goals, but it's easier to understand everything we'll talk about later if you work through some hypothetical numbers with me now.

It's called The Rule of 72.

It's not exact. It doesn't take into account specific goals or tax situations or total assets. It is, however, a great benchmark that has been around longer than I have—in fact, I have friends who were taught this rule by their parents.

To figure out how to make your money double, decide how quickly you want it to double in years, and divide 72 by that number.

If you want to double your money in 7 years, divide 72 by 7 and you get 10.3. Your money has to earn 10.3 percent a year for the next 7 years in order to double.

If you want to double your money in 6 years, divide 72 by 6 and you get 12. Your money has to earn 12 percent a year for the next 6 years in order to double. It's the awesome power of compounding.

Keep that in mind—we'll come back to that number. Let's do a couple of examples and then you can do your numbers.

Work back from your goal. Want to stop working at age 50? Good for you! How old are you now? 30? You have 20 years to save up enough to stop working.

What will you need?

Watch me turn $60,000 into a million bucks

Let's say you like your current lifestyle: a new car every three years, a nice house, movies, dining out, a weekly round of golf with friends. Retirement should never be about skimping; it should be about enjoying the rewards. Write down what you have to earn today to maintain that lifestyle. Are you able to enjoy that life on $50,000 a year? $75,000? $100,000? Put down the number that's true for you.

Let's use $75,000 for our example. "If I can have $75,000 a year coming in every year starting when I'm 50, I won't have to worry." But that's your current gross income before taxes. When you're retired and you're not paying Social Security taxes and you're in a lower tax bracket, you don't need to earn $75,000 to make the same net income. Also, if you've paid off your mortgage, you don't need that extra $1,000 a month in mortgage payments. A good rule of thumb (again, just a generalization— who knows what inflation rates will be?) is that you'll need 80 percent of your current salary.

So, to continue with our example, 80 percent of $75,000 is $60,000. You want $60,000 coming in. You need to have accumulated enough capital to be returning you $60,000 a year without having to touch the principal.

Are you a conservative person? If you don't want to worry about that principal disappearing you're going to put it in very safe investments. These days, the most conservative investments (such as CDs) earn about 6 percent a year. So, how much principal would you need to earn you $60,000 a year at 6 percent? $1 million (6 percent of $1 million is $60,000). If you're a person who can tolerate slightly more risk so that money earns 8 percent a year, you'd need $750,000 in capital to produce $60,000 a year in interest.

Stay with the higher figure. Call it $1 million. That's right. You saw it. A million bucks! It's time to start investing! (But watch the magic of compounding: I'm going to turn $60,000 into a million.)

Back to The Rule of 72.

If you currently have $60,000 and you want to build it to about $1 million in 20 years, it's got to slightly more than double every 5 years (5 years: $120,000; 10 years: $240,000; 15 years: $480,000; 20 years: $960,000).

According to The Rule of 72, for your money to double every 5 years it's got to earn 14.4 percent a year. If your current nest egg of $60,000 grew at an annual rate of return of 14.4 percent, it would grow to that $960,000 in 20 years.

At 14.4 percent, you can turn $60,000 into $1 million in 20 years without contributing a penny more. If you can contribute more as you go, you'll hit that $1 million even faster.

Now it's your turn. Let's do a worksheet based on a retirement plan. Most financial service providers have a place on their Web site where you can enter your numbers and it will do these calculations for you.

Okay, here's where it gets a little harder to explain, because this number is different for every person and there are three variables—the amount you have on hand, the amount you want it to grow to, and the length of time you want it to take. The simplest way to do it is this: Take the number you got in question 3. Divide it in half. Divide it in half again.

Target Number Worksheet

1. **I currently have $** _____ **available for investment.**
   (Remember, zero times anything is still zero, so start putting something away.)

2. **In order to enjoy my retirement and live the way I'm living now, I need an annual income of** _____ **$.**
   (About 80% of your current gross income or the gross income you'd like to have.)

3. **In order to generate that amount of money in interest income on a yearly basis, at 6% interest, I would need the folllowing capital investment: $** _____ .
   (To determine this number: Take the number you entered in Item 2 and divide by 6, then multiply by 100.)

4. **I want to be ready to retire in** _____ **years.**

Keep dividing it in half until it's close to the number you got in question 1. Using our earlier example of $60,000 (for question 1) and $1 million (for question 3):

$1 million ÷ 2 = $500,000.

$500,000 ÷ 2 = $250,000.

$250,000 ÷ 2 = $125,000.

$125,000 ÷ 2 = $ 62,500.

In our example, we had to divide $1 million in half 4 times to get close to $60,000. For your specific needs, you might have to do it 3 times or 5 times or more.

Divide the number of years you wrote in question 4 by the number of times you divided. If you wrote down 20 years in question 4 and then divided $1 million in half 4 times, then you divide 20 by 4 and get 5. This is the number of years your money has to double each time. Divide 72 by that number to get your percentage rate (72 divided by 5 = 14.4). That's the percentage rate your money has to earn to reach your goal.

That's your target number. Keep it with you for the rest of this book.

After you start managing your money against your own goals, review it at least twice a year.

Remember I told you that over time, investing in the stock market has historically been the best way to increase your money? Over the past 20 years, money invested in the stock market has grown at an annual rate of return of about 16 percent. (And that's counting the 20+ percent return of some recent years.) If you're like most people I know, your number x was probably a lot higher than 16 percent.

To give you an idea of how different the last few years have been, compare the following annual returns based on different portfolio holdings:

	Last 3 Years	Last 20 Years
100% Growth Stocks Portfolio	24%	18%
100% Value Stocks Portfolio	13%	15%
100% All Stocks Average Portfolio	22%	16%

These growth stock returns of the past three years are extraordinary. Will they continue? No one knows, but if you're new (or late) to investing, don't worry that you've missed the boat. Remember, you're still out there working. Every month (or even better every week), you're going to be adding to that nest egg—and that new money will start to go to work for you as well.

A number of financial service providers will let you crank the planning numbers online. You can enter your current assets, your annual contribution, the final goal, and the number of years you have to get there. A program will immediately calculate what your annual rate of return needs to be to reach that goal.

Why did we do this exercise? So the rest of the book will make sense. If you know stocks have historically returned about 16 percent and you know what percentage you need to have, you can start to shape your financial strategy. Aggressive? Conservative? Balanced? Aggressive for the first five years?

You can also compare each year's results with your goals. Your online account should give you a percentage summary instantly. With that information and your own number in mind, online investing can help you sharpen and clarify your plans and goals:

> **WHAT A DIFFERENCE A DAY MAKES.**
>
> On Black Monday, October 19, 1987, the Dow Jones Industrial Average plunged by 22.6 percent, far more than the 12.9 percent drop in 1929 that kicked off the Great Depression. No wonder people got nervous. What a lot of people tend to forget is that the day after Black Monday, the market posted an all-time record gain of 102.27 points. That record was shattered two days later with a 186.64 point gain. By September 1989, the market had recouped the entire loss. It proves a point I'll make more than once in this book: The stock market rewards the patient, long-term investor.

- Every six months, compare the actual rate of growth of your account with the number in your goal.

- Adjust your targets for the coming time periods based on those results.

- Compare your results each year with your peer group (aggressive investors, conservative investors) and review your investment allocation (you'll learn how in Chapter 11).

- Did your investments do better? Worse?

Keep your number in mind as we go through the different types of investments. Start to jot down ideas in the margins: types of securities you want to consider, rates of return that make sense to you, and degrees of risk you can tolerate.

Go with your gut. If something sounds good but you're uncomfortable, listen to yourself. What good is a potential 28 percent return on an investment if you're tossing, turning, and terrified you're going to lose all your money?

At the end of the book, flip back through the pages and summarize all your notes. That's your personal guide to online investing.

Never forget *it's your money.*

If you're not in control of your financial future, who is?

Step III:

Meet the Street

Wall Street Fundamentals

It's a multitrillion-dollar business. It involves every nation on the planet. It can all be explained in three sentences:

1. Someone wants your money and will offer you something in return for it.

2. Return is measured in two ways: return on investment and rate of return.

3. The greater the risk, the greater the potential return.

The details can fill a library—or the Internet:

1. Someone wants your money and will offer you something in return for it.

- "Someone" could be a global corporation, a local company, a utility, the federal government, a fund manager, a local municipality, a regional planning authority, a state government, a start-up company, or your brother-in-law.

- To get you to invest your money, they'll create some kind of financial instrument or security (a general term for anything that can be bought, sold, or traded) such as a stock, bond, or mutual fund (all of which we'll explain later).

- They'll almost always tell you what they'll do with your money before you have to put it up. The federal government needs to pay for all the services it provides that cost more than the taxes we pay. A city might want to improve its schools or build a stadium. A regional planning authority could build a mass transit system. A utility might need a new plant. A corporation could be looking to invest overseas, acquire another company, or refinance their old debt.

A fund manager might want to put your money in *all* of those alternatives. Your brother-in-law might want to buy some old 45s he saw in someone's basement so he can sell them for a profit.

❝The biggest misconception is that people will make large amounts of money in a very short period of time when they first start out. It takes time to educate yourself and learn how the markets operate.❞

E.P., Physician

2. Return is measured in two ways:

- **Return on investment** is the amount your money grows or declines. If you invest $1,000 and you end up with $1,100, you had a $100 return on investment. If you invest $1,000 and sell out at $900 you lost $100 on your investment.

- **Rate of return** is expressed as a percentage. It's the return on investment divided by the length of time (usually measured in years) it took to earn that return. If you invest $1,000 and you take out $1,100 a year later, you had a 10 percent *annual* return on your investment. If you invest $1,000 and take out $1,100 just six months later, you had a 10 percent return on investment, but that equals a 20 percent return on an annualized basis.

Much of your research will be about trying to estimate the rate of return and return on investment, but that equals a 20 percent return on an annualized basis.

3. The greater the risk, the greater the potential return.

There are some exceptions. But it's a good rule to keep in mind. Here are some examples:

- If you lend your money to a bank for three months or more by buying a **Certificate of Deposit** (CD), you're going to get a relatively low interest rate. The money, however, is just about as safe as anything in this world: It's insured by the federal government (up to $100,000), so if the bank goes belly up, the government will see that you get your money back.

- If you lend your money to a business that's just getting started (a start-up company), the risk is high—and so is the potential reward. You might never see a dime of it again or you might be in on the ground floor of the greatest company ever created. High risk, high reward.

MONEY MAKES THE WORLD GO 'ROUND

Companies. Governments. Utilities. These examples are just a fraction of the different types of borrowers and a fraction of the different ways to put your money to work. They're basic examples of the reason why all financial markets exist: to match buyers to sellers for every form of financing that's possible. And if you really want to lend money to your brother-in-law, make sure you get it in writing and get a decent return on your investment or know what you want in return.

certificate of deposit (CD)
Money on deposit with a bank for a fixed amount of time in exchange for a higher rate of interest than a regular savings account.

Most investment information is meant to help everyone assess the amount of risk versus the potential value of the reward. That's it. The rest of the financial world is just variations on the ways your money can go to work for you and the different degrees of risk.

CD LOW INTEREST RATE?

It's not a compact disc, it's a Certificate of Deposit. The flip side of "The greater the risk, the greater the potential reward" is "The lower the risk, the lower the potential reward." If you're curious about the lowest interest rate someone can offer and still get takers, check out the current rates on bank CDs.

Start with
Stocks

Stocks: A Form of Ownership

Ever wish you owned a company you've heard about? Every time you buy a stock, that's what you're buying. Here's how it works:

An entrepreneur—let's call her Jill—has a great idea that she thinks just can't fail, so she decides to start a business. After all those years of working for someone else, it's her turn. Good for her! Problem is, at some point she's going to need money to make it grow. That money is called *capital*. (Why do you think we're called capitalists?) No one is just going to hand it to her; she has to go out and raise it.

Jill can raise capital all sorts of ways: Use the money she inherited from Grandma. Cash in her life savings. Max out the cash advance limits on all of her credit cards. Borrow from family and friends. Take out a second mortgage on her house. Jill can also forego a salary, live on peanut butter and the charity of her spouse, and plow every cent she gets back into her growing business.

Let's say Jill can't settle for the kind of chump change she could raise on her own. She needs megabucks. So, she decides to offer other people the opportunity to buy a piece of her business. They'll *share* in the profits and they'll *share* in the losses—because they'll own a *share* of the company (that's why stocks are also called shares).

When a company issues stock, they're inviting people to own a piece of their business. The first time Jill offers shares of her company to the public is called an Initial Public Offering (IPO). There are investment bankers and companies whose sole job is to help private companies *go public* (sell their shares to the public for the first time). Take that growing business of Jill's. Initially, she owns 100 percent of the company, but she needs a whole lot of cash (or capital in kind) to get it going, more than she could possibly raise on her own. So, she decides to raise money by selling (issuing) stock.

Let's say Jill offers to sell 50 percent of the company to the public in shares worth 1/2 percent each. She sets the price of these shares (*price per share*) at $750 each. She's saying her company is worth $150,000. The half she sold to the public is worth $75,000 ($750 x 100 shares) and the half she owns is worth $75,000.

The good news? Jill still owns half the company and she's raised $75,000 in working capital. The bad news? The people who own the other half literally own half her business. They're entitled to half of her profits—and they take the risk of sharing half of her losses. Because they own (*hold*) shares in her company, they get to talk to her at least once a year (at the annual shareholder's meeting) and publicly praise or blame her for the job she's doing.

Two more concepts will give you the basics of stocks. What if Jill offers people those 100 shares at $750 a share and no one wants them? They may not want them for one

START ME UP!

Before a young company can even consider going public, it needs to establish a business, start earning revenues, and build a strong position in the marketplace. So where does the money come from in those early stages? Entrepreneurs often exchange part of their growing businesses to a special breed of investors called venture capitalists (also known as "VCs"). In exchange for a piece of the company, venture capitalists invest their money and often lend expert guidance to entrepreneurs. Wealthy individual investors who provide capital to start-up companies are called angel investors. These high stakes forms of investing are extremely risky—but the prize is the potential for extremely high returns if the company goes public and becomes successful.

of two reasons: The price per share is too high or the value per share is too high.

At $750 a share, someone who wanted to buy 100 shares would have to pony up the whole $75,000. Not only would it cost that person a lot of money, but Jill would now have one partner with an equal voice in her business. So, instead of issuing 100 shares at $750, Jill decides to issue 1,000 shares at $75. By doing this, she makes the shares affordable—but now each share is only worth .05 percent of the company instead of .5 percent. (The total number of shares times the share price has to equal the total value of the company. Because Jill has issued 10 times as much stock, each share has to be worth one-tenth as much. If you bought 10 shares at $75 [$750] you would own the same 1/2 percent you'd have owned if you'd bought 1 share at $750.)

By issuing a larger number of shares, Jill is able to keep the price per share low enough to be attractive to investors. But what if no one wants to buy those shares even at the lower price? It's probably because the value of the shares (and the company) is set too high.

Just because Jill thinks half her company is worth $75,000 doesn't mean the rest of the world agrees with her. When she sells the stock, she could ask $75 a share for those 1,000 shares, but the public might only bid $70—they've set a **market value** of $70. In effect, they think Jill's company is worth only $140,000, not the $150,000 she was asking.

market value
The price at which a stock can be bought or sold based on the value investors apply to the company.

Is it really that simple? Pretty much, except the numbers are larger. When you're talking about Microsoft or Ford Motor Company or General Electric, you're talking about tens of millions of shares. But the principle's the same. The people who run the company are trying to maximize the value of the shares of stock you own by making smart business decisions. Other people like yourself are buying and selling (trading) shares in those companies.

What Happens to the Stock when a Company Is Doing Well?

A number of things are possible:

1. The stock may increase in value. If the company does very well, people will probably increase their estimation of the value of that company. Your shares will most likely increase in value because people will be willing to pay more per share to own a company that's doing better than when you first bought the shares.

2. Companies that pay dividends will distribute a portion of the profits to shareholders. If the company has 10 million shares and earned $12 million in profits that year, their *earnings per share* were $1.20. They could pay that to each shareholder at the company's discretion, declaring a dividend. If you owned 100 shares, you would get a dividend check of $120 in the mail (or a disbursement credited to your account).

3. The stock may split. Despite what it sounds like, it's actually a good thing. If the price of a single share becomes too expensive (as in our $750-a-share example), a company might increase the number of shares available. If you owned 1 share that was equal to 1/2 percent of the company's value and the company decided to double the shares available, they would issue a 2-for-1 stock split. With no extra work on your part, you would now own 2 shares— each worth 1/4 percent. The total value would still be the same, but the price of the shares would be cut in half. Now, the stock price is lower and both your shares would increase as the stock price increases. A $1 increase in 1 share translates to a $2 overall increase if you own 2 shares. This is getting good, right?

What Happens to the Stock if a Company Doesn't Do Well?

A number of things might happen:

1. No dividends. The company posts (announces) an unplanned loss for the quarter or fiscal year. They don't have any profits to distribute, so you won't get any dividends. The only good news here is that, although you can put money in your pocket if the company does well (in the form of dividends), you won't be called on to chip in to cover its losses (except perhaps in the form of a lower value in your stock holdings).

2. The value of the company will probably go down. The public probably may not want to own shares in this company. And even if they do, they probably won't want to pay as much as you did. So, even though you paid $75 a share, you might find yourself with shares worth only $60. What should you do? Usually, nothing. Remember, you're in this for the long haul, and most large companies won't abide losses over long periods of time.

REMEMBER CHRYSLER

Once upon a time, Chrysler Corporation was facing bankruptcy. Outmoded plants. Outmoded cars. The president of Chrysler at the time, Lee Iacocca, asked the federal government for a loan to keep Chrysler going. At the time, if you owned shares in Chrysler, the bad news had pushed the price per share way down. If you trusted Lee to fix the problems, however, you made the right choice—today, you'd be the proud owner of a large number of shares in Daimler Chrysler.

3. Reverse splits and buy backs. Just as a stock can split 2 for 1, it can do the opposite, called a reverse stock split, and go down to 1 share for every 2. Another common situation is a buy back. If a company feels the public doesn't value it as highly as it values itself, it might buy back some shares of the company. This reduces the number of shares outstanding and (sometimes) raises the price of those outstanding shares.

4. Mergers and acquisitions. If the value of the stock goes down too far, the company might become ripe for a merger, acquisition, or takeover (sometimes friendly, sometimes hostile). The company's managers might look for a *white knight* to buy the company. If another corporation was interested in acquiring the company, it would try to buy all outstanding shares from stockholders (tender an offer). Once this announcement is made, another corporation might also want to enter the bidding.

Finally, just as there are different types of companies, there are also different types of stocks. The two you'll come across most often are **common stock** and preferred stock, and they mean exactly that. Preferred stock is a class of stock that gets preferential treatment. What that preference is varies from company to company, and often a large company will issue different types of preferred stocks. Don't worry about this too much. Most companies issue only common stock.

Do you like the idea of stocks? You should. They're the most powerful investment tool ever created. As I said before, investing in stocks is the best way to significantly build your capital over a long period of time, but even late-blooming investors can benefit from the potential growth in stock.

As an online investor, you can research and find company stocks that match your investment goals—once you know what you're looking for and how to look for it. What are some factors?

common stock
Publicly-traded shares of a company. They give the owner an ability to attend the annual shareholders meeting. If the company goes out of business, owners of common stock get paid after creditors and preferred stockholders.

Size Can Matter

Big caps, growth stocks, mid caps; when you consider buying a stock, you shouldn't be interested in just price. You should also be interested in the size of the company.

How big is big business? Wall Street measures companies the way we measured that hypothetical $150,000 business. Simply multiply the number of shares outstanding (always available with a little research) times the share price. A company with 10 million shares outstanding at $63 a share is said to have a **market capitalization** of $630 million. Using that formula, Wall Street classifies companies into three broad categories: big (or large) cap (capitalization), mid cap, or small cap.

market cap
A way of measuring the size of a company by multiplying its current share price by the number of shares outstanding.

What's a big cap stock? A company that has a market cap in excess of $10 billion—as much as Bill Gates or the Sultan of Brunei—but they're not companies. Big caps are businesses such as Cisco, Boeing, Kodak, General Motors, Intel, and Microsoft.

Mid caps range from $1 billion to $10 billion—companies such as Pixar, Scotts, and Medarex. Small caps are valued at less than $1 billion and are often not as well known: Bindley Western, Cell Genesys, and Strategic Diagnostics to name three you've probably never heard of.

And when it comes to buying stock, you're not just restricted to American companies. Stocks in some big, mid, and small cap overseas corporations such as Volkswagen, Ericsson, and Nokia trade on the U.S. stock market as well. A practical way for Americans to invest in these stocks is either through a mutual fund that specializes in offshore companies, or by purchasing American Depository Receipts (ADRs), which are shares in overseas companies issued by a U.S. bank and traded domestically.

Quality Counts

Ever hear the term *blue-chip companies*? These are companies that, year after year, generally deliver solid, reliable performance—a good return on investment. In general, blue-chip companies are all big cap, although not all big caps are blue chip. Just because a business is big doesn't mean it's healthy.

Growth Is Important

Growth stocks aren't those strange things in the back of your refrigerator. It's the term for a company that's growing fast: Its revenues are projected to grow even faster than in the past; often these companies pay little or no dividends on profits, but rather pour them back into the business. Sometimes growth stocks could be in companies such as Xerox and IBM in the 1950s and 1960s. Sometimes an entire category of stocks become growth stocks—such as Internet stocks in the late 1990s. The key to successful investing in growth stocks is timing: knowing when to get in and knowing when to get out.

Some people believe that mid and small cap stocks tend to grow faster (although usually with some dips along the way) than big caps because they generally have more room for revenue expansion.

"Stocks sound great, where can I buy some?"

Currently, stocks are traded in one of three ways: on an exchange or "auction" market, in the over-the-counter (OTC) market, or via an ECN (Electronic Communications Network). (Although this stuff is important to know, you don't need to memorize it. Your financial service provider will route your order to the appropriate market.)

- An exchange is a place such as the New York Stock Exchange (NYSE), the American Stock Exchange (AMEX), and various other regional exchanges such as the Philadelphia Stock Exchange and the Pacific Stock Exchange. The NYSE (also called "The Big Board"—those New Yorkers love to brag) is the oldest and largest of the stock exchanges, and it's where you'll find most of the oldest and largest blue-chip and big cap companies. Exchanges function as a mass auction between buyers and sellers. All orders are funneled through a single location where a specialist manages the auction process. Prices are based on supply and demand. You've seen those pictures on TV with traders scurrying around the floor filling orders. Orders on an exchange are filled using what's known as open outcry.

NO EXCHANGES, NO RETURNS. The history of the different stock exchanges makes for fascinating reading. It won't necessarily make you a better investor, but you'll sound smart at the next meeting of your investment club. You can visit the Web sites of these different exchanges, but all you'll get there is the pasteurized version. For the juicy stuff, you'll find some suggested reading in the bibliography.

WARNING: CHECK YOUR BULLETIN BOARD

As you investigate different stocks and opportunities, you might come across bulletin board stocks (also frequently referred to as penny stocks). These are over-the-counter stocks that are not included in the NASDAQ daily listings. Although you can trade bulletin board stocks online, this market is less automated than the listed OTC market, with lots of human intervention from the market makers. Consequently, the prices that appear online are considered nominal quotes (not necessarily representative of the price you would receive). Be very cautious. These stocks are speculative in nature.

- The over-the-counter market is an association of independent market-makers connected by computer networks who openly compete with each other for buy and sell orders on the NASDAQ (National Association of Security Dealers Quotation System) where most new technology and Internet companies appear. The market-makers hold inventories of the stock and execute transactions on your behalf.

- ECNs are the latest thing. They allow you to trade shares before, during and after market hours (after the close or before the open) without going through an exchange or market-maker. ECNs match up buyers and sellers, automatically making the "exchange" and executing the order. Until very recently, trading this way was restricted to just the big boys—market-makers and large institutional investors.

E*TRADE, like all good financial service providers, provides real-time quotes for securities traded in all of these markets.

Market Indexes

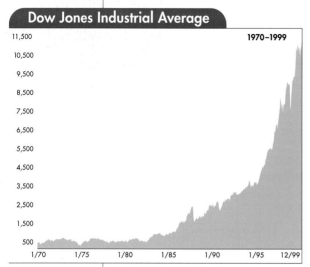

Dow Jones Industrial Average

1970–1999

11,500
10,500
9,500
8,500
7,500
6,500
5,500
4,500
3,500
2,500
1,500
500

1/70 1/75 1/80 1/85 1/90 1/95 12/99

Ed Koch, the "Mayor for life of New York City" (his words, not mine), used to ask reporters "How'm I doing?" It's a question every investor wants to know.

How do your stocks stack up against everyone else's? Are you doing better than the general economy? Worse? Should you be taking more risks or fewer?

Market indexes track the up and down price movements of groups of individual stocks and the market as a whole. Analysts use them to measure conditions in the market and the economy. You can use them to help with your decisions about which securities to buy, sell, or hold and to measure how the stocks you own are doing compared with others.

Each index is made up of a group of securities considered to be representative in gauging which way market and economic winds are blowing.

The nation's oldest and most closely watched market indicator is the Dow Jones Industrial Average (DJIA or "the Dow"). It's made up of the 30 bluest of the blue-chip stocks, most on the NYSE, that theoretically represent the backbone of corporate America. Among them are Boeing, Disney, Eastman Kodak, General Motors, Hewlett-Packard, McDonald's, Microsoft, and Wal-Mart Stores.

The second oldest and most closely watched market indicator is the Standard & Poor's 500 Index (S&P 500), which tracks 400 industrial, 60 transportation and utility, and 40 financial stocks (listed on the NYSE, AMEX, and NASDAQ) that are viewed as industry leaders. The 500 companies aren't always the biggest, but they're a mix of publicly traded companies in areas most vital to the U.S. economy. Because of this, many market watchers believe the averages of the

"WHAT'S GOOD FOR GENERAL MOTORS IS GOOD FOR THE COUNTRY."

That celebrated quote by Charles Erwin Wilson, the former head of General Motors, was made in 1952 to the Senate Armed Services Committee. Is it true? The Dow uses only 30 companies to reflect the entire economy. It's sometimes criticized for not being broad enough to be a fair cross-sampling of all stocks. The recent (1999) addition of Microsoft and Intel to the Dow is an attempt to address that criticism and keep the Dow current.

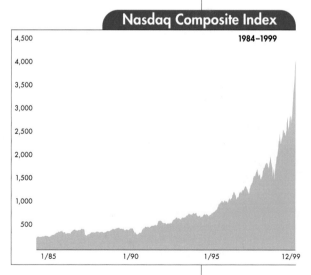

Nasdaq Composite Index

1984–1999

4,500
4,000
3,500
3,000
2,500
2,000
1,500
1,000
500

1/85 1/90 1/95 12/99

A Day in the Life of Nasdaq

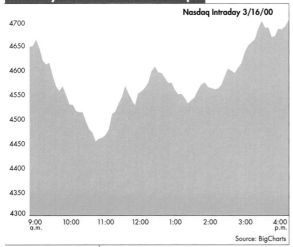

Nasdaq Intraday 3/16/00

Source: BigCharts

The Rollercoaster
These days, it's not unusual for the Dow or Nasdaq to fluctuate 100 points or more within a single market day. Just a few years ago, this kind of volatility would have been considered noteworthy but today it's just part of how the market works.

S&P 500 are a more accurate barometer of broader market performance and trends than the DJIA.

The Nasdaq Composite Index tracks the performance of the OTC market. It's made up of many emerging company stocks and some well-established technology goliaths such as Intel and Microsoft listed on Nasdaq's national market and small cap market. Many analysts say this index is the most representative indicator of trends in the much broader, more speculative small cap market.

Other popular indicators used by traders and analysts include:

The Value Line Composite Index tracks the performance of about 1,700 NYSE, AMEX, and OTC stocks that are typically nearest and dearest to the hearts (and in the portfolios) of the average investor. Analysts consider it to be the most accurate gauge of average investor feelings about the market.

The Wilshire 5000 Total Market Index tracks the movement of "all U.S. headquartered equity securities with readily available price data." Analysts say it's the broadest trend indicator of all.

The New York Stock Exchange Composite Index tracks the ebb and flow of every security listed and traded on the "big board."

The Russell 2000 tracks the broad performance of smaller cap stocks. Put aside the 1,000 largest companies trading in the U.S., and the Russell 2000 tracks the next 2,000 largest publicly traded companies.

At E*TRADE and at a number of other financial informa-tion sites, you can follow the daily averages of any of the key indexes online. And as an advanced trader, you can chart the movements of specific stocks against other stocks on these key indexes, taking your own barometric readings with a variety of easy-to-use market indicators and analytical tools (see Chapter 17: Stock Investing 2.0 and Chapter 18: Let's Talk Trends).

"Okay, Christos, how do I turn that information into investment decisions?"

What was the target number you worked out in Chapter Six? 12 percent? 18½ percent? 23 percent? That number will guide you to the stocks you want.

- Is your number lower than the stock market's current rate of return? Then you can be looking at solid, slow-growth companies, possibly blue-chip big cap.
- Is your number close to the market's current rate of return? Then you can be looking at the stocks the indexes are tracking.
- Is your number higher than the market's current rate of return? Then you've got to hunt out small cap opportu-nities or high-growth stocks.

It only has meaning in the context of your own plan.

CHAPTER 8

Bonds.
Treasury Bonds.
Corporate Bonds.
Muni Bonds.

Bonds: A Form of Debt

Stocks are a form of ownership. Bonds are the equivalent of a loan—from the bondholder (that's you) to the bond issuer (that's the company). If, historically, investing in stocks has been the best way to significantly build your capital over a long period of time, then why would anyone want to invest in bonds? Because the bond issuer is obligated to pay you interest, you get a predicable income flow from your investment. Bonds can be attractive when you're at a stage in your investment life when current income is more important than future equity growth. Bonds also offer some insurance against swings in the value of stocks (although bonds can be volatile, too, and carry the risk of capital loss, as we'll see). Once you know something about bonds, you should be able to make informed decisions about their place in your portfolio.

Governments have to borrow money to do what they want. Sometimes companies do, too. But instead of going to a bank, governments and companies ask investors to lend them money that they agree to repay with interest. How much interest they pay is directly related to point number 3 in the Meet the Street section: the greater the risk, the greater the potential return.

Just about anyone can issue bonds. Cities and counties issue municipal bonds to finance large projects that need to be paid for before the tax revenue comes in (mass transit, new schools, ballparks). Utilities issue bonds to pay for new plant or power line construction. Companies issue corporate bonds to pay for expansion or capital improvement.

The federal government does it all the time (Treasury bonds and Treasury bills). You know those savings bonds your parents bought for your college education? Your parents were lending the federal government money, and the government agreed to pay it back with interest.

Having the federal government owe you money is a pretty good deal. The United States federal government has never defaulted (failed to pay back) on any of its loans. And it doesn't look like it's going out of business anytime soon. Lending your money to the United States is considered just about the safest investment you can make—so the interest they pay is pretty low.

If you buy a corporate bond, on the other hand, you've got other factors to consider: How stable is the company? Who's running it? How good are the products they make? How much cash flow do they have? How much other debt do they have? What will the money be used for? Are these general bonds or for specific activities? Investment bankers who help the company issue the bonds take all this into account and try to set an interest rate that's as low as possible (to keep the company happy) yet still high enough to attract investors.

How do you buy and sell bonds? It used to be a tricky process involving a bunch of phone calls and paper forms, but thanks to the efforts of E*TRADE and some savvy bond experts, a revolution has taken place in the way bonds are sold. Today, you can buy bonds pretty much the same way you buy stocks—by logging onto your online investing account, researching and selecting the bonds you want, then placing an order. Not all online financial service providers offer this service, so if bonds are important to you, take a close look at what your provider offers.

Because bonds are debt, they're usually issued in denominations of at least $1,000 in increments ranging from $1,000 to $5,000 and more.

How does a bondholder get paid? In general, you receive your interest payments from the issuer in semi-annual installments (called coupons) until the loan comes due and the debt is satisfied (the face value is repaid).

Bonds are a fixed-income security—they return a fixed rate of interest income. If you buy a $1,000 bond that pays 8 percent interest, you'll get $80 each year for as long as the bond exists—and then $1,000 back from the borrower at maturity. You know it. They know it. There's a sense of stability and control with bonds. When you buy a bond, the issuer agrees to repay the full amount of the loan at a specific time—the bond's date of maturity.

THE MARK OF ZERO

Zero Coupon Bonds are discounted from their *face value* against the interest they yield. If a $1,000 bond pays 8 percent interest and returns $1,080, a $1,000 Zero Coupon Bond would cost $926 and pay $1,000 at the end of the year—paying you 8 percent on your initial investment. Zero Coupon Bonds are a clever and effective way for people to buy high-yielding bonds at a discount.

Boring? Hardly. Once a company or government issues a bond, it can be resold, possibly many times. The issuer doesn't care who owns it or what they paid for it. They issued the bond for a fixed amount (the *face* or *par value*) to be repaid at a fixed time in the future to whoever owns it. Because bonds are traded, it makes for some interesting possibilities.

Take a look at today's interest rates (they should be on your financial service provider's Web site). They affect the value of your bonds: Generally, when interest rates go up the value of bonds goes down and when interest rates go down the value of bonds goes up. Why? Because the interest payments on bonds are fixed.

Imagine you have a $1,000 bond that pays 8 percent. You paid $1,000 for it a year ago and it matures in five years. The interest rate of the bond is close to the general interest rate at the time it was issued. Why? Because it's a loan. If a company or government wants to borrow money, they're looking for the best deal. If they can borrow money more cheaply from someone else, why should they offer you bonds? The bond rate is going to be competitive with the prevailing interest rates. Always. And that's the key to understanding them.

Back to that 8 percent bond. A year has passed. The prevailing interest rate is now 10 percent (not really, this is just an example). A bond issued today would pay 10 percent interest. If you wanted to sell your 8 percent bond and not hold it to maturity, why would anyone want it? If they can get 10 percent from new bonds, why should they pay you $1,000 to get 8 percent?

They won't. But if they offered you $800 for your bond, they'd be making 10 percent on their investment.

"Huh? Run that by me again?"

If someone pays $800 for an 8 percent bond that has a face value of $1,000, the issuer still pays the holder $80 interest. The holder is making the equivalent of 10 percent return on their investment ($80 is 10 percent of $800).

This is what we mean when we talk about a discounted bond: Its face value on the street (as in "Wall Street"— another term for the stock market) has been discounted so that the interest an investor earns will be competitive with prevailing interest rates.

"But what if interest rates go down?" you ask.

Good news for bondhold-ers. You could buy a bond with

> **GETTING OFF TAX-FREE**
> Tax Free Bonds are exactly that—the government that issues the bonds says it won't charge you taxes on the interest you earn on their bonds. Of course, that applies only to the people who live in that location and only to that level of government.

Bond Quick Picks

Below are lists of current bond offerings, pre-sorted for your convenience and available for immediate execution.

Treasuries
- Active Treasuries
- Bills
- Notes, 0 to 1 Year
- Notes, 1 to 2 Year
- Notes, 2 to 4 Year
- Notes, 4 to 7 Year
- Bonds, 7 to 15 Year
- Bonds, 15 to 30 Year

Treasury Strips
- Strips, 0 to 6 Year
- Strips, 6 to 12 Year
- Strips, 12 to 22 Year
- Strips, 22 to 27 Year
- Strips, 27 to 30 Year

Live Municipals
- Live Municipals

Live Corporates
- Focus List
- Globals
- Financial
- Industrial
- Telephone & Utility
- 0–5 Year
- 5–10 Year
- 10–30 Year

Agencies
- Thru 12/01
- 1/02–12/04
- 1/05–30 Years
- Zeros

Zeros
- Treasury Strips
- Agency Zeros
- CATS, ETRS, TIGRS

an 8.75 percent coupon, and the prevailing interest rate (the best interest rate available to large borrowers) could drop to 5.75 percent. The payers on that 8.75 percent bond have to pay much higher interest than the current rate. This also means that someone would probably be willing to buy the bond from you at greater than par value; they might give you $1,200 for the bond because the greater premiums would offset the higher price.

This brings me to the subject of callable bonds. A callable bond is just what it sounds like: The issuers reserve the right to call it back at a certain date. If they can pay it off early, or can borrow the money cheaper at a later point in time, they can buy back the bonds and save themselves some money.

When you research a bond, you're likely to see a call date associated with it. This is the date when the issuer can say, "That's it, here's your money, the loan's off." It's an important thing to keep in mind if you were planning to hold that bond for the next 25 years.

YIELD AHEAD

How do bond traders measure the return on a bond? With four different yields: nominal yield, current yield, yield to call, and yield to maturity.

The **nominal yield** is the value of the bond based on when it was issued. If a bond was issued at 8 percent; that's the nominal yield.

The **current yield** is the yield relative to its current market price. It's the rate of return you'd get right now. If a $1,000 8 percent bond is selling for $800, its current yield is 10 percent.

The **yield to call** is the yield from right now until the call date, if there is one.

And the **yield to maturity** is the yield you'd get if you bought the bond now and held it until the due date when it matured.

Bonds Give You a Measure of Control over Your Portfolio

You don't know if your stocks are going to go up or go down. You don't know if interest rates are going to go up or go down. You don't know if your stocks will pay dividends. But you do know (to a degree) what a bond is going to pay. You can take a percentage of your assets and lock in a guaranteed rate. If you buy a ten-year Treasury bond paying 7 percent, you now know that portion of your money will definitely earn that amount of return for that length of time.

The bond market in the United States is huge compared with the stock market, even though there are just two major categories of issuers: the government (federal, state, local) and corporations. The largest government issuer of public debt is—you guessed it—the U. S. Treasury. All their bonds (and there are hundreds of different ones with different interest rates and different dates of maturity) are generally referred to as Treasury securities. But don't let the "securities" part of the name fool you. Whether issued by a government or corporation, a bond is either secured or unsecured (yes, it's possible to have an unsecured security—just as it's possible to be unsociable on Social Security).

A secured bond is backed by specific assets of the issuer, which can be sold off to pay you back if the issuer fails to pay its obligations. Mortgage-backed bonds are an example of a secured bond: the bond is backed (guaranteed) by the mortgages of people like you.

Unsecured bonds (also called debentures) are backed only by the full faith and credit of the borrower. In other words, there's no real collateral. There's nothing backing these bonds except a promise that they'll be paid back. Gulp? Depends on who's doing the promising. U.S. Treasury bonds (T-bonds for short) are unsecured bonds—but no one worries too much about whether the U.S. government will default. Most corporate bonds are unsecured.

WHY PAY TAXES?

The big attraction of municipal bonds is that if you live in the state in which they're registered, you'll avoid paying some taxes on the interest (coupon) payments (up to a certain amount, under what's called the alternative minimum tax). It's a great way to shelter future income from tax payments.

PUT IT ON MY TAB

The reason the bond market is so much larger than the stock market is the same reason you've got so much debt on your credit card. A company can sell only so much of itself. It can't offer the public more than 100 percent of itself. But there's no limit (in theory) to the amount of money a company can borrow. Plus, governments can't issue stock. If a city, state, or federal government needs more money than it's got, its only choice is to borrow (or raise taxes! just kidding).

"Okay, Christos, but how can I tell if a company is solvent?"

Two independent companies—Standard & Poor's (S&P) (*www.standardandpoors.com*) and Moody's (*www.moodys.com*) —do it for you. They monitor the world of public debt and

BUY YOUR OWN HOUSE

Ever have a mortgage? Ever notice that the bank issuing the mortgage isn't the same company that asks for your payment each month? That's because banks "sell" your mortgage to investment companies. They put a whole bunch of mortgages together and create mortgage-backed bonds that they sell to people like you. So if you own mortgage-backed bonds and have a mortgage, you can pretend that when you write a check to the mortgage company each month, some of that money is coming right back to you through your mortgage-backed bonds.

JUNK, ANYONE?

In the 1980s, investment bankers created a bond that was so risky that services such as Standard & Poor's wouldn't even rate them. They became known as junk bonds. The name alone gives you the chills. A junk bond might work like this: The management of a company decides to buy the company back from the public. They issue bonds that are used to buy all the outstanding stock. These bonds are backed only by the company's ability to make money. Of course, the company is now saddled with this huge debt (the interest on these unsecured bonds), making it almost impossible for the company to reinvest in itself, raise new capital, or compete in the global marketplace. Hence the term junk. For a chilling account of junk bonds at their best, there's still no better tale than the book *Den of Thieves* by James B. Stewart.

grade the caliber of bond issuers for fiscal strength and debt-paying reliability.

High caliber bonds—bonds whose issuers are considered reliable and financially stable—are called *investment grade*. In general, the higher a bond's rating, the higher the investment grade and the lower the interest it pays. The lower a bond's rating, the lower the investment grade and the riskier the investment and the higher its interest rate will need to be to attract investors.

Because Treasury bonds are free of default risk (After all, if the government can't pay off its bonds, it just prints more money. Don't you wish you could do that?), Treasury bonds are considered to be the highest quality bonds available. As a result, they're not rated. Instead, they're used as the benchmark against which all other bonds are rated and priced.

E∗TRADE's Bond Center provides the S&P quality rating for millions of bonds. Make sure the financial service provider you're considering does that as well.

"So, Christos, what do I do with that information?"

Now you've got a choice. Do you want to share in a company's risks and potential rewards as a stockholder—or do you want to have it owe you money as a bondholder?

As a stockholder, you could watch the value of your stock go up or plummet to nothing. As a bondholder, your returns are generally less volatile, and if the company goes bust, you're first in line to be paid off ahead of the stockholders. They're sharing the risks, while you're holding an I.O.U. One of their risks is that they'll have to pay your I.O.U. One of your risks is that the company might go belly up. Following the rule that the greater the risk, the greater the (potential) reward, you should get a higher rate of interest from a company that shows any signs that it might not survive long enough to pay you back.

The answer's in your plan and your number.

If your money is all in stocks, you live and die by market forces. Was your target number (the annual percentage rate at which your money has to grow to meet your goal) higher than the current stock market rate of return? In that case, you might want to take an aggressive position in stocks to reach your goals. On the other hand, you don't want to put all your capital at risk. Faced with this problem, some investors put a percentage of their money in bonds with a fixed rate of return. They're protecting themselves financially (hedging). If the high-return, high-risk stocks don't perform well, they're balanced by medium-risk, medium-return bonds (or low-return, low-risk bonds) to protect their capital and keep it working.

Was your target number lower than the current stock

HOW SAFE CAN YOU GET?

Some people believe U.S. government Treasury bills (T-bills) are the safest security of all. Like Treasury bonds, they're issued to the public at a guaranteed rate of interest. They're sold at a discount from their face value in minimum denominations of $1,000 to a maximum of $1 million. The difference between the discounted price you pay for a T-bill and its face value is your return. Interest isn't paid to investors until the T-bill reaches maturity in either 3, 6, or 12 months, at which time you get the face value—you would pay $926 for a 12-month 8 percent $1,000 T-bill and then get paid $1,000 when the year is up.

Bond Credit Ratings

S&P Rating	Definition
AAA	The highest quality, lowest risk bonds.
AA	High quality debt obligations with minimal repayment risk.
A	Quality bonds with a strong capacity to pay interest and principal but somewhat susceptible to adverse economic conditions.
BBB	Quality bonds with adequate capacity to pay interest and principal but more vulnerable to adverse economic conditions.
BB	Medium-grade bonds with few desirable characteristics.
B	Speculative bonds with a major degree of risk in adverse economic conditions.
CCC	Issuers in poor standing.
CC	Issuers may be in default.
C	Income bonds on which no interest is being paid.
D	Bonds in default.

market rate of return? Some investors see this as a signal to build capital in a less risky position. They might want a higher portion of their capital to be in low- to medium-risk bonds to keep their money growing without exposing it to unnecessary risk.

HAVING YOUR CAKE AND EATING IT TOO

Can't make up your mind between stocks and bonds? Want to move between being a shareholder and a bondholder? You can do that. It's called a convertible security, or a convertible bond. It's a type of investment that allows the owner to convert his/her holdings to another security. For example, corporate bonds converted to shares of the company's stock, or preferred stock to common stock. Although this might sound like the best of both worlds, it can also turn out to be the worst of both worlds—no equity and low returns on the debt.

Was your target number the same as the current stock market rate of return? When their investment program seems to be right on schedule, some investors try a balanced strategy of mixed risk: a percentage of money in low-risk to medium-risk bonds, a percentage of money in blue-chip stocks, and a percentage in higher-risk stocks or bonds. They adjust the percentages according to their own tolerance for risk. Some investors increase the risk quotient a little, figuring that if they're wrong, they haven't hurt themselves over the long term. And if they're right, they can reach their goals that much faster.

Your Plan. Your Goals.

So what'll it be—stocks or bonds? Or stocks and bonds? The decision is yours and the tools to help you make that decision are online.

CHAPTER 9

Funds, Funds, Funds

Mutual Funds: A Form of Shared Risk

One of the fundamentals of smart financial planning is diversification. To help manage your risk, you want a mix of different types of securities (stocks and bonds) and a mix of different individual securities in each category. That's fine if you've got a spare $100,000 to start with. What if you're starting smaller and want to get that mix right away? You could buy *odd lots* (any amount not divisible by 100 shares) of different stocks or heavily discounted bonds or T-bills; or you could invest in a mutual fund.

In a mutual fund, money is pooled from a number of investors and a fund manager invests it in a diversified mix of stocks, bonds, or other investment vehicles, depending on the objective of the fund. In other words, when you buy into a

SHARE AND SHARE ALIKE

In general, stocks are sold in *round lots* (units) of 100 shares. If a stock is selling at $62 and you want to purchase one round lot, you'll pay $6,200 plus your commission (if any). You can purchase more or fewer than 100 shares, of course, and any purchase that is not in multiples of 100 is called an *odd lot*. There's really nothing odd about buying 80 shares or 138 shares. I think it's just a catchy phrase invented by stockbrokers to make customers feel embarrassed about buying fewer than 100 shares, but you shouldn't feel embarrassed at all. In fact, buying your niece or nephew or son or daughter one or two shares in different companies they might have heard about (such as Sega or Nike or Disney for example) can spark a lifelong interest in and knowledge of managing their own finances.

mutual fund, you're actually purchasing shares, or pieces, of a portfolio (mix of securities) that could contain any number of different stocks and/or other securities depending upon what type of mutual fund it is. If the value of one security in the fund plunges for a time but the value of the other securities remains constant, you take less of a hit because the value of the overall fund remains stable.

It doesn't necessarily take a lot of money to buy into a mutual fund. Many funds will allow you to start purchasing shares for an initial investment as low as $250.

The fund manager selects the securities in which the fund invests; makes all buy, sell, or hold decisions; and charges a percentage of the fund's net asset value (the current value, calculated at the end of each market day, of one share of the fund) for doing so.

The fund manager is guided in his or her decisions by the fund's objective, which is defined in its *prospectus*—a detailed account of the fund's goals and strategies, past performance, transaction costs (if any), expenses, and other financial information the fund company is required by SEC regulation to disclose to mutual fund shoppers.

Prospectuses can be obtained directly from the fund company. Or E*TRADE makes the prospectuses of more than 5,000 mutual funds available online.

"But what if I don't like their strategy?"

Invest in a different fund. Fund managers, recognizing that different investors have different objectives, have become increasingly sophisticated in designing funds to cater to a wide variety of investment needs and styles.

For example, the objective of an income fund might be

OTHER PEOPLE'S MONEY

A mutual fund manager is a professional investment manager who's spent his or her career studying the markets and different types of securities. Unlike a broker who simply helps you (for a fee) buy and sell, a fund manager is more like a mother hen: carefully tending all the eggs in the basket to make sure there are no rotten ones. Because mutual funds can have as much as tens of billions of dollars in shared assets, mutual fund management has become a high-profile profession in the past 10 years. Every year, financial magazines and online services rank different fund managers, comparing their results to the Dow. When investing in a fund, you should consider: Who are the managers? How long have they been managing the fund? and What have their results been in the past?

short-term income rather than capital growth, while the objective of a growth fund is capital appreciation. An aggressive growth fund strives for maximum capital appreciation (with associated risks). The objective of a growth and income fund is both capital appreciation and current income. Bond funds are mutual funds that invest exclusively in bonds (government or corporate).

A *stock mutual fund* invests only in stocks, but there are different types of stock funds. For example, an *index fund* invests only in the securities of a particular market index such as the S&P 500. *Emerging growth funds* invest in new technologies or new companies that are just starting up and growing fast. Keep in mind that mutual funds, like stocks and bonds, are subject to the same risk/reward rule. An aggressive growth fund would be more volatile (subject to the ups and downs of the market) than a less-aggressive one.

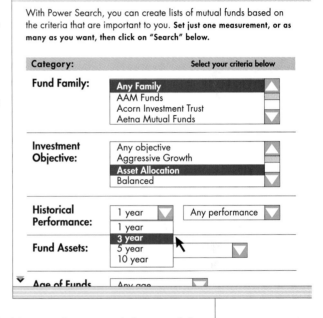

An *international mutual fund* invests strictly in foreign company stocks whereas a global mutual fund invests in both U.S. and foreign company stocks. An *emerging markets mutual fund* invests mainly in the equities of companies in developing economies.

A *money market fund* consists of lower-risk investments such as U.S. Treasury bills, bank certificates of deposit, and short-term corporate or government bonds with fixed interest rates; it's often used as a low-return harbor for extra cash that's waiting for the right investment opportunity to come along.

All in the Family

These days, just about every fund is part of a fund family— a group of funds of different types, with different objectives, offered by the same mutual fund company. In general, you can move your money from one fund to another fund within the same fund family without any penalties, additional fees, or commissions.

POLITICALLY CORRECT

The extraordinary range of stocks and bonds combined with the variety of possible combinations has made for some very interesting mutual funds: You can find funds that match your political, philosophical, or ideological beliefs. Looking for a fund that only invests in environmentally correct companies? You can find it. A fund that buys companies that subscribe to Christian beliefs? They're out there. It's an interesting way to put your money where your mouth is.

It's a smart way for a mutual fund company to keep you a customer for life: At the outset, you can diversify your fund holdings by dividing your nest egg among a number of different funds. Then, as your investment strategies and needs change over time, you can change your ratio of risk to reward or move into specialized funds to take advantage of changing market conditions. Make sure you reappraise your objectives and your fund's (and fund family's) performance quarterly. Just because one fund in a family is doing well doesn't mean they all are.

Where do you find mutual funds? Online, of course. Good online financial service providers have resources that can guide you to finding a fund that matches your investment goals.

Want to Get Loaded?

Have you seen any commercials about *no-load funds*? What's a load? What's a no-load fund? A *load* is like a membership fee for a club—it's what they charge either to get in (a *front-end load*) or to get out (a *back-end load*). No-load funds don't charge these amounts, but they may have higher management or expense fees associated with them. How can you tell? Research, research, research—online financial service providers have the tools to answer those questions and more.

Innovations in Mutual Funds

With so many new companies coming into the marketplace and so much demand for a wide range of investment choices, mutual fund companies and financial service providers have recently been getting more creative. By the end of 1999, there were 3,008 stock funds to choose from in the U.S. Many of the newer mutual funds are investing in emerging technology stocks or micro-cap stocks and are based on indexes covering unique portions of the technology or international sectors. Soon, we'll be seeing the equivalent of personal mutual funds based on automated trading of groups of securities according to your personal profile and financial plan.

"Okay, Christos, how do I know where funds fit in my financial future?"

What's your target number? How much money do you have to invest initially? Although past performance is no guarantee of future results, you can track a mutual fund's performance long term—and it could be a simple way for you to find a diversified mix of stocks and bonds that match your goals. In Chapter 14 we'll talk more about what to look for in determining whether a fund can match your goals.

CHAPTER 10

Where to Stash Your Cash

It's 10 P.M. Do You Know Where Your Cash Is?

C ash is a slacker. I'm talking about the stuff in your wallet. In your cookie jar. Under your mattress. Sitting idly in a non-interest-earning checking account waiting for you to take it out at the next ATM you pass. That stuff doesn't earn interest and doesn't grow (in fact, in an inflationary economy, cash actually "shrinks").

However, cash can also be a liquid asset, by which I mean money that's earning interest and can be converted quickly to cash. There are a lot of reasons you might want to have that:

Security. Most financial planning books tell you to have up to six months of living expenses in cash, in case you want to change jobs or your boss tells you to. That money should be earning interest for you.

Expenses. Sometimes we know we're going to need a large chunk of cash in a couple of months: college tuition, wedding, vacation. That money should be earning interest for you.

Diversification. As part of your diversification strategy, you might want to have a percentage of money in cash. That money should be earning interest for you.

Shifting Investments. This is often the most common form of investment cash—money that's sitting around while you decide what you want to invest in next. That money should be earning interest for you, too.

Once you start thinking about cash as a liquid asset, you can start reassessing where you keep it, how you use it, and how hard it's working for you. Online, you've got more choices than ever, including financial service providers such as E*TRADE, which can offer full-service banking as well.

Online Banking

What Are You Getting?

Have you looked at the interest rate you're getting, if any, on your bank deposits? There's a reason why many of the tallest, most extravagant skyscrapers dotting skylines throughout the world are owned by banks. Until recently, banks have operated in an industry where the barriers to entry are high and existing cost structures have kept out competitors and enabled behemoths to thrive. Although this status quo has been great for the banks, you and I have fronted the costs.

Fortunately, the same revolution that created online investing is driving online banking, as well. Think about this: In 1989, only about 3 percent of all banking transactions were done outside of brick and mortar. By the end of 1999, nearly 65 percent of all banking transactions were done via PC, phone, or ATM. Although perhaps not as engaging or complex as online investing, online banking offers some special advantages. The one significant advantage online banks provide is a dramatically reduced cost structure that can lead to greater benefits for you.

Online Banking Basics

Checking Accounts. Say good-bye to a lot of extra fees. With a minimum balance, such as $1,000 or more, online banks offer very competitive rates, along with free checking, ATM and debit cards, and 24-hour online access to your account information. More often, traditional banks charge for these services. Increasingly, online banks are also offering free bill payment services connected to your checking account.

Savings Accounts. A savings account with an online bank can earn you "super premium yields"—nearly double the rate of brick-and-mortar savings accounts. And just as in an old-fashioned bank, your money is insured by the federal government (FDIC) up to $100,000.

Bank Certificates of Deposit. These are short-term, medium-term and long-term interest-bearing notes issued by online banks as well as traditional banks. Like a savings account, they're insured by the federal government up to $100,000. In general, a 30-, 60-, or 90-day CD will pay higher interest than a savings account because you're locking your money up for a period of time. It can be a smart place to put money you know you're going to need in a specific length of time. CD rates from an online bank such as E*TRADE Bank are generally within the top 1 percent of all rates around the country.

Online Bill Payment

Payee	Amount	Transmit Date	Category
FNAC	$590.00	1/27/2000	Car Payment
VISA	$720.00	1/27/2000	Credit Card

Be sure to schedule the transmission to allow sufficient time for your payee to receive the payment. Payments scheduled for transmission on non-business days are transmitted the next business day.

PAY BILLS >   RESET

Bill Presentment and Payment. Does anyone enjoy paying bills? Online bill presentment and payment can eliminate the grind of writing out checks, hunting for stamps, and manually balancing your checkbook. More and more online financial service companies are offering the ability for you to both receive and pay bills from your checking or money market account. Check the cost. Some online financial service providers charge for bill payment and presentment services and some are now offering this service for free when you maintain a checking account with a minimum balance.

Virtually Full Service. Just like traditional banks, a number of online banks now offer a full range of financial services including auto loans, consumer lending, mortgages and insurance.

Liquid Assets Between Investments

Money Market Funds

You've decided to hold some money out of the stock market and don't want to buy bonds. How do you keep your money safe, earn higher than savings bank interest, and yet keep that money readily available for a quick move into an investment? The simple answer is money market funds.

Virtually every online financial service provider offers money market funds. They're a smart way to keep your money safe, earn interest that's higher than a traditional savings bank pays, and yet be readily available for a quick move into an investment. Money market funds are a smart place to "park" your money, but make sure you know where you're putting it—and why. After all, when you're invested in a money market fund you're really looking for safety first. There are four key points to be aware of with these funds:

1. Your funds will not be government insured. Although I know of no default of a money market fund that has cost investors their money, and certainly none is seen on the horizon, you could possibly lose all or part of your principal. If you're worried enough about the economy or the fund's backers to think default, put your money in the bank.

2. Like other funds, a money market fund is selling shares. The difference is that this fund has made you the promise to maintain a $1 per share value on the shares you buy. You'll pay no buy or sell fees and you can sell your shares for the $1 value at any time. What you'll get for that $1 investment is a higher interest from the money market fund than you would in an ordinary savings account.

How is that possible? Because the fund you've invested in will take your money (and that of all its other investors) and buy the highest quality government and commercial grade fixed-income investments it can, and it will share those returns with you in the form of higher interest. In short, you benefit from the fund's size and expertise in the fixed income market.

3. Almost every money market fund will give you check writing privileges. The number of checks that you can write each month (from fewer than three to possibly even an unlimited number) and the minimum amount for which you can write a check (from more than $500 down to 1¢) may vary. Check it out.

4. Money market funds come in several types. The three most popular are:

- **Taxable**, no minimum on the invested amount.
- **Taxable with a minimum investment required.** This type of fund will earn you even higher levels of interest.
- **Nontaxable** (state and local taxes). This type of fund generates a lower level of interest, but that interest is free of state and local taxes. If you live in a high tax state such as New York and you are in a high income

tax bracket, your net return from one of these funds may be higher than that in a taxable account.

If your money market fund account is part of an investing account family, as you buy and sell investments the money will be freely transferred between your money market fund and your other investments, seamlessly. This is a great feature that saves time, hassle, and money.

In general, money market funds, which were invented in the 1970s, are an extraordinary money management feature that provide a high level of safety, a high level of interest earned, and a flexibility that can't be matched. As you look at putting your money in a money market fund, analyze the type of fund, its interest rate return, its flexibility, and how convenient it is for you. The only real downside of a money market fund has to do with your money management discipline. Because the money is so easy to move into investments or spend, you need to be sure of your financial goals and use the money to foster those goals both short and long term.

> **KEEP YOUR MONEY AT HOME**
> Although many banks offer money market products, it's smart to look for money market funds run by your financial service provider. As you move money between investments, you can automatically put your uninvested funds into a money market fund, so your money's always earning interest. E*TRADE, for example, offers eight different types of money market funds.

CHAPTER 11

Know
Thyself

H ow was your weekend of bungee jumping? Did you have a good time? Ready to risk your money in the same way? I thought not. In Chapter 6, I talked about making a plan. Now that you understand more about different types of investments, you need to look at that plan with an eye to risk.

Here's the key point: It doesn't matter what your level of risk is. What matters is your comfort level. If you can't stand risking your principal, you're never going to be comfortable with a high-risk stock investment. You'll nervously check the online quotes at every opportunity and you'll want to sell at the first sign of even a modest setback in your investment's performance. Dump Chrysler in the 1970s? Bad call over the long term. The temptation to run at the first sign of trouble can be harmful to your bank account, your long-term financial goals, and your stomach lining.

How Much Risk Can You Tolerate?

It's as important a question as "what's your target number?". You might need to pursue an aggressive investment strategy —but you might also have a conservative stomach.

Conservative risk-takers are likely to define risk as potential loss of their principal. Concerned more about safety than anything else, they're more willing to accept a lower rate of return in exchange for a lower degree of risk. This may translate into choosing securities, such as fixed-income investments like bonds, whose value may slip a bit during a downturn in that particular market but will likely bounce back over the long haul.

More aggressive risk-takers are less willing to tie up too much money over long periods in low-yielding, fixed-income investments, preferring the faster, bigger potential returns the riskier stock market may offer. Anytime your money is in play, it's always at some risk. The more informed and prepared you are, the better positioned you are to mitigate the risk—but there are no guarantees.

Financial advisors and experienced traders add that your degree of risk tolerance can change over time as you approach certain goals. A young, single investor can usually take more risks than an older, married investor who's nearing retirement.

Assessing your investing personality—whether you're a conservative risk-taker, an aggressive risk-taker, or some-where in between—can be an important component in sizing up potential investments. And just as there are dif-ferent kinds of investments, there are also different kinds of risks.

Key Types of Risk

Interest Rate Risk. When the cost of borrowing money goes up (often due to fear of inflation), it eats away at the value of certain types of investments. This hurts the most if you're in long-term fixed securities. If you bought a bond with the "fantastic" rate of 8 percent, and five years later interest rates move above 8 percent, you either have to sell your bonds for a loss or continue to earn a not-so-fantastic percentage less than prevailing rates.

Investor Psychology. Overreaction to fluctuating interest rates and inflation fears by panicky investors prompts a market *sell-off* that affects the value of investments, even among those who kept their heads. If you like to "go with the herd," then you'll be susceptible to this form of risk.

Liquidity. A liquidity risk is the inability to convert an investment quickly and easily to cash when needed without incurring a significant loss in the value of the investment. Remember our discussion about cash? Don't let yourself get caught in a place where you can't convert securities into the money you need.

Market Conditions. Stock prices can soar to such highs per dollar invested that the market and your individual investments become more vulnerable in the event of a decline. This is also referred to as market volatility—large, frequent swings in the indexes. If you're always looking for an excuse to buy or sell, you'll be vulnerable to market conditions.

IF

"If you can keep your head when all about you Are losing theirs and blaming it on you . . .

Yours is the Earth and everything that's in it,

And—which is more—you'll be a Man my son!"

Remember having to learn that poem by Rudyard Kipling? You didn't know he was writing about securities investing, did you? It's tough to hang in there when the crowd's rushing the other way, but often it's exactly the right strategy—if you can handle the risk.

Does Investing Online Lessen the Risk of Losing Money?

Only to the extent that it puts all the tools and resources in your hands to conveniently make your own investing decisions. When you're online, you can easily scan the market indicators, size up the markets, and track movements and prices—giving you a personal "feel" for what the economy and the markets are doing. In that sense, being online makes you a "professional fund manager"—but the fund you're managing is your own portfolio. Online investing gives you the power to act on the information you gather.

Managing Risk

Do you have to be clairvoyant? Are all those risks beyond your control? Smart investors know two good strategies that can help mitigate the effects of most risks.

Asset Allocation, or Spreading Your Eggs Around

I've said it, every professional money manager says it, and it's worth repeating: To safeguard your portfolio against the various types of risks, diversify. Don't put all your eggs (investment dollars) in one basket (a single security or investment sector).

Spreading your investments among stocks, bonds, mutual funds and risk-free cash equivalents lessens the chance that a poor showing by one of them will jeopardize the overall performance of your portfolio and increases the odds that you'll get the returns you need to meet your investment goals.

This broadly accepted strategy for **hedging risk** is referred to as diversification, or asset allocation. Whatever names it goes by, however, it adds up to this: Strength lies in variety and numbers.

Although no strategy can guarantee success, history has shown that a balanced portfolio is less vulnerable to enemy attack from investment risk because not all types of securities do well, or poorly, at the same time.

Asset allocation strategies take advantage of this unwritten law by averaging out your risk of market volatility. In fact, many analysts believe that the percentage you assign to each investment sector has even more of an impact on your portfolio's overall returns than the specific stocks, bonds, or funds you choose. The weight you give each sector should be re-evaluated and shifted as you move

UP AND DOWN AND DOWN AND UP

Different securities move in different directions at the same time. For example, when interest rates go up, bond prices generally go down. But over the years, whole markets show different behaviors. In 1967 the government bond market plummeted almost 10 percent (the worst downturn in that market in 60 years), while the market in small cap stocks rose 83 percent (its best showing in more than two decades). When the stock market dropped 28 percent in October 1987, foreign bond markets jumped 16 percent the same month. When the Asian economy went south in 1997, we reciprocated: The American markets were largely unchanged and the U.S. economic engine sustained world growth until Asia recovered.

hedging risk
An investment activity or strategy designed to reduce risk. Sometimes portfolios reduce the risk of loss by using one investment (such as an option— see Chapter 16) to offset another.

GIVE IT TO ME BY THE NUMBERS

The rules vary, but for those of you who are looking for something to hang your portfolio on, here's an example of how a financial planner might suggest allocating your assets:

**Early-Life Investors
(Running with the Wolves)**

Stocks or stock funds:	75%
Bonds or bond funds:	15%
Money markets:	10%

**Mid-Life Investors
(Running with the Herd)**

Stocks or stock funds:	50%
Bonds or bond funds:	25%
Money markets:	25%

**Late-Life Investors
(Take the Money and Run)**

Stocks or stock funds:	25%
Bonds or bond funds:	50%
Money markets:	25%

NOTE: Dollar cost averaging won't protect you from a bad investment. You still need to monitor it.

through different stages of your life and career. Being a self-directed investor, you have to come up with your own personalized formula, taking your individual goals, assets, income level, investment preferences, and personal and family circumstances into account. Investing online gives you resources to make, review, and revise your asset allocation decisions.

Dollar Cost Averaging

Dollar cost averaging is a powerful investment tool that can help you manage your risk for any form of investing, and it's a smart way to get you into the habit of saving small amounts regularly. Say you have $12,000 to invest. If a security you're interested in is trading at $10 a share in January, your $12,000 will buy you 1,200 shares. But with a dollar cost averaging strategy, you instead buy $1,000 worth every month. Take a look at this simple chart (assuming some hypothetical movements in the price):

Month	Investment Amount	Share Price	# of Shares
January	$ 1,000	$ 10	100
February	$ 1,000	$ 8.50	117.6
March	$ 1,000	$ 9.00	111.1
April	$ 1,000	$ 10	100
May	$ 1,000	$ 10.50	95.2
June	$ 1,000	$ 11	90.9
July	$ 1,000	$ 10.50	95.2
August	$ 1,000	$ 10	100
September	$ 1,000	$ 9.75	102.6
October	$ 1,000	$ 9.50	105.3
November	$ 1,000	$ 9.50	105.3
December	$ 1,000	$ 9.25	108.1
Year	$12,000	$ 9.79	1,231.3

Using dollar cost averaging, at the end of the year you own 1,231.3 shares at an average price of $9.79. If you'd just bought 1,200 shares in January, you'd have paid more on average for fewer shares. And even though the security's down to $9.25 a share in December, you're only down $663.12 instead of the $750 you'd be down if you'd spent the full $12,000 in January. You reduce your risk and increase your ownership at the same time!

If you don't feel you fully understand the basics of:

- Your Personal Financial Goals
- Stocks
- Bonds
- Mutual Funds
- Money Markets
- Your Personal Risk Comfort Level

Don't go any further. Go back and re-read any section you're not familiar with. Let me repeat a point I made before: Online investing is a form of investing in which you, the investor, have control of your actions, your research, your information, your decisions, and your own account—it's not a form of gambling. *Investing without knowing what you're doing is a form of gambling* whether you do it through a full-service broker, a discount broker, a bank, or an online account.

Re-read any sections you don't understand until you understand what they mean, why you need to know them, and how they can serve you in your quest for financial independence. *If you're still not clear about what you're doing, you're still gambling.* Once you're sure about what you're doing, then let's . . .

Ready to join the revolution? This is what online trading & investing is all about.

Here it is. You've got a computer, a modem, an ISP, a financial service provider, an online account, and a plan. You, as an individual—sitting in your home, your office, or in your car on your cell phone—now have the power to do more research and gather more information than at any other time in the history of the world.

How you research, where you research, what you research, knowing why you research: Those are the keys to taking control of your own finances—and they're the key to getting the most out of online investing.

A great online financial service provider will help provide insight on *how* you research and *where* you research. They'll have up-to-the-minute breaking news you can tune into, vast stores of historical data you can check out, access to fellow investors and market professionals, and research and analysis tools that can help you sort through investments and find the ones that best fit your needs.

What you research is entirely up to you—and it's just about the most fun you can have in taking control of your financial future, because now you're an *online investor.* Whatever your goals, whatever your strategies, you now have new ways to explore and uncover the investment opportunity that's right for you.

- **Your current financial goals help define your search.** If you're a 20-something college grad, there's probably not much point in researching the different rates on 30-year Treasury bonds—something that might be of more interest to a 50-something baby boomer.

  You're an online investor. Focus your research on the types of financial instruments you want. You've made your plan and you know your number, so you can hone in on investments and strategies that can help you hit your target.

- **What puts you on the path of a new opportunity?** You're watching television and see a commercial for a new drug, Viagra. Sounds like it could be a winner.

  You're an online investor. You go online and find out the name of the company that manufactures it, Pfizer, and its ticker symbol (PFE). You do your research and make the decision to add a small position to your portfolio.

- **Your doctor told you about a gold mine stock he's investing in.** Hmmm. Has he already told the last 240 patients he saw—and who told him?

  You're an online investor. You no longer have to take those "tips." Go home, research the stock he's talking about, then e-mail him a message telling him what you've found out and why it's a crummy investment. He'll sell out his shares—and he might even make a house call the next time you're sick.

- **One day you get a call.** It's your old stockbroker—or some stockbroker who fished your name off your subscription copy to *People.* She's got a "can't lose" investment opportunity (even though you know there's no such thing).

You're an online investor. You go online, enter the stock symbol, do the research, and know whether the broker spoke the honest truth or just wants to earn a commission.

- **At the family picnic,** Aunt Libby, a keen mutual fund investor, is raving about the returns she's been getting on a new high tech mutual fund she recently invested in. Do you run home and blindly move all your money into that fund?

  You're an online investor. You look up the fund symbol, bring up the fund profile and take a look at the fund's investment objectives and top ten holdings. From there you review the fund's full prospectus and decide, based on your target number, your portfolio, and your research, whether or not to invest and, if so, just what percentage of your portfolio you should invest in this particular opportunity.

It's all around you.

Get it? You're a living, breathing, walking financial analyst. In your daily routines, you come across dozens of opportunities that can translate into smart or not so smart investments. You've got the power to make the decision for yourself because you've got the power of the Internet.

You're an online investor.

Step IV:

You've Got the Power

CHAPTER 12

Online Stock Investing

N ow some of this is going to be fun and some of this is going to be like work...real hard work! But if you're going to take control of your own financial future, you've got to do your homework. The online revolution has given us the "emancipation of information," yet the only way for you to turn this valuable information into personal empowerment is by knowing how to gather, analyze, and interpret it to help meet your own goals.

❝I was paying my full-commission broker outrageous prices. Online investing made it easier (and cheaper) for me to trade with less aggravation; and I don't have to argue with my broker.**❞**

K.D., Online Investor

What You Can Do Online

- **Analyze** stocks of your choice in any particular market sector or index.
- **Chart** the performance of a stock over a specific time period.
- **Compare** the pricing information of one stock against another.
- **Research** a company's financial background and profit picture.
- **Watch** what the markets, what professional analysts, and what investors like you have to say about a

particular stock.

- **Listen** for signs of movement in the markets.
- **Read** just about any recent news reports about a particular company or sector.

Why? Because it all plays a part in deciding whether a stock meets your financial goals and is right for you. But before you do the research, you need to understand what you're looking for—and what it means when you find it!

Look at your target number.

Always start with what you know—which is the number you're going for and the amount of risk you can tolerate. As you uncover investment opportunities that seem to match your needs, start to compare them using some key indicators to sort them out and make your choices. As you put it together with your financial goals, your risk tolerance level, and your common sense, you're on the way to putting together a financial portfolio that works for you.

How?

The same way you shop for *anything* you need.

Sizing Up a Stock

Your goal is clear: you're trying to find stocks that are going to go up in value. Detailed company profiles and financial data such as income statements, annual and quarterly balance sheets, annual cash flow, and dividend and split histories can all help you in your mission and are all available online. Start with some of the more fundamental financial data, key measurements, and ratios to assess the potential risks and rewards of investing in a particular stock.

THE BIG MO

Sometimes by the time you get a lead, momentum players (professional traders, day traders) have already driven up the price of a stock. They've gotten out and moved on. But there you are looking to just get in and get started. Don't let the hype (and a recent run up) distract you—do your research.

1. Find a Lead. TheStreet.com, Briefing.com, CBS Marketwatch, CNN, CNBC, ClearStation.com, Bloomberg News, RedHerring.com, *The Wall Street*

Journal, Barrons, your great uncle Fred. In the news, on TV, on the radio, and online—there's no shortage of financial information. Pay attention to what they're saying and combine that with what you know. Soon enough, you'll start uncovering leads on your own.

2. Look It Up. Once you've identified a company you want to investigate, look it up. How? Either by the name or the ticker symbol (It's a unique set of initials, generally an abbreviation of the company's name, such as INTC [for Intel Corporation], WMT [for Wal-Mart] or BA [for Boeing Aircraft]).

Every online financial service provider allows you to get a current stock quote. In the box that says Enter Names or Symbols, enter either the name of the company or its ticker symbol. Then click "Go." Immediately, you'll see a page that shows you the latest stock quote and a host of additional information. All of this is useful in helping you determine whether that security is the right investment for you.

3. Get a Price Quote. There are two kinds of quotes (current prices) you can find on most good financial Web sites these days: delayed quotes and real-time quotes.

- **Delayed quotes** (generally delayed 15-20 minutes) used to be the fastest the public could find anything out on the market. In fact, it used to take almost that long to get an order filled in the old days before the online revolution—brokers would have to move paper around and call the order in over the phone before anything would happen. The question is this: Do you want to be 20 minutes behind the market? Things can happen in a matter of seconds when the markets are active—if you wait that long, you can miss out. A 20-minute delayed quote is like yesterday's paper— leave it in the kitty litter box. Check the fine print:

When you're looking up a quote, somewhere on the page should be a time stamp indicating when the quote was reported by the exchange.

- **A real-time quote** is the last reported price information on that security. It's hot, it's up to the minute, and it lets you know what's happening right here and now. Because this is valuable information, most, if not all, sites providing this information will ask you to complete an exchange agreement indicating that you are accessing the data for personal use only. Some may charge extra for this valuable service.

4. Study the Data. When you get a detailed quote, you really get a detailed profile of the security you selected. This set of data is a close-up snapshot of current performance and trading history—giving you a lot of the information we've talked about:

WHERE DOES IT TRADE AND WHY DO I CARE?

We get a lot of questions about listed stocks and NASDAQ/OTC stocks. How do you tell the difference? It's easy—just check out the symbol. Stocks with symbols that are *three letters or fewer* (such as T, BA, or IBM) are listed stocks—they trade on either the NYSE, the AMEX, or on the regional exchanges. Stocks with symbols that are four letters or longer (such as MSFT, INTC, ERICY) trade on the NASDAQ/OTC (over-the-counter). Should you care? Not really, but now they're easier to find.

Reading a Detailed Stock Quote Online

Box	What It Means
price	The price at which the stock last traded (could have been a purchase or a sale).
change	The amount that the security's price changed from yesterday's closing price to today's current price.
bid	The highest price anyone will pay for the stock.
bid size	The number of shares that are currently available at the bid price.
ask	The lowest price anyone will offer the stock for.
ask size	The number of shares that are currently available at the ask price.
open	The price at which the stock first traded when the market opened.
volume	The number of shares of the stock traded so far that day.
day range	The highest and lowest price investors paid or sold the stock for so far that day.

EPS	Earnings per share. The total earnings of the company divided by the number of outstanding shares (see explanation that follows).
tick	Up or down movement of the security's price between the last trade and the one just before that. An uptick (+) indicates the price is higher; a downtick (-) indicates that the price has dropped.
P/E	Price-to-earnings ratio is a measurement of how much the stock is selling for divided by the company's annual earnings (see following)
52-wk high/low	The highest and lowest prices paid for the security during the past 52 weeks. The range between the two numbers indicates the security's volatility, a measurement of its short-term risk of ownership.

Study all this closely. What price is the stock currently trading at? How does it compare with other stocks in the same industry and other stocks in your portfolio? Then move on to other key factors that can help you decide whether to buy, sell or hold.

Detailed Quote

EBAY INC (EBAY)
January 31, 2000 3:49 PM ET   Real-time quote, NASDAQ NM

Price	**$150^1{}_{16}$**	**Change**	**+2$^1{}_2$ (+1.69%)**
Bid	150 +	**Ask**	$150^1{}_{16}$
Bid Size	400	**Ask Size**	800
Volume	2,035,000	**Tick**	up
Day range	145–$152^5{}_8$	**Open**	146
EPS	0.08	**P/E**	1875.78
52wk Hi	234 (4/27/1999)	**52wk Lo**	64 (2/10/1999)

5. Study the Basics.

Everyone wants to know someone who's in the know. You've heard cool investors talk about market caps and P/E ratios. You can too. Most investors look at three basic measurements to determine the fundamental value of any company. Of course, there are plenty more you can look at—and we cover those in Chapter 17; but these are the most common ways to get a quick look at a company's worth: market capitalization, earnings per share (EPS), and price-to-earnings ratio (P/E).

MARKET CAPITALIZATION

What Is Market Capitalization?

Remember when we talked about big cap, mid cap, and

small cap companies? This is the figure that measures a company's size and financial strength. Market cap describes the value that investors have ascribed to a given company.

How Can I Determine Market Capitalization?

It's calculated by multiplying the current price of a stock by the number of shares outstanding on the market. So, if 1 million shares are outstanding and the share price is $50, the market capitalization is $50 million.

Why Do I Care About Market Capitalization?

In theory at least, the biggest, most powerful market-leading companies will have the largest market capitalization. Accordingly, buying stock in a big cap company is usually viewed as a more conservative, less risky investment. Buying into General Electric, with a market capitalization of roughly $440 billion, could be viewed as a safer investment than 1-800-FLOWERS, with a market capitalization of around $440 million (roughly 1,000 times smaller).

EARNINGS PER SHARE (EPS)

What Is EPS?

If you owned a company with three of your friends, you would expect to take home one-fourth of the company's profits. Earnings per share is the same idea: It describes how much income is credited to your piece of a company, that is, what you're going to make as the "owner" of a business for every share you own.

How Do I Determine Earnings per Share?

Earnings per share is net income per share of the company's common stock after taxes, depreciation allowances, potential losses, payments to holders of preferred stock and bonds, and other costs have been deducted. If that's too much to remember, think of it as earnings minus some

MIRROR, MIRROR ON THE WALL, WHO'S GOT THE BEST PROJECTED EARNINGS OF ALL?

Following each quarter, companies announce their earnings for that period, and, quite often, their projected earnings (what they hope they're going to make) for the remainder of the year. Industry analysts make huge amounts of money trying to guess what that number will be before the company announces it. When you read the daily financial information on the Net, you'll often find predictions from analysts—along with disclaimers from company management. A company generally looks good to the stock market if they beat the analysts' projections—even by a few pennies! (Remember, a nickel a share times 10 million shares and you're talking real money: $500,000 to be exact.)

costs divided by the number of shares outstanding. For example, if the company has 1 million shares of common stock outstanding and nets $1million in a year, its EPS would be $1 for that year. Hypothetically speaking, if you owned 100 shares and the company closed up shop with its $1 million earnings in the bank, you would actually get a $100 slice of the pie from the company. (Assuming the company had no debt or preferred shareholders.)

What Does This Mean for Me?

If the company's EPS is up from the previous year, this may indicate the company's in good fiscal shape with profits on the rise.

PRICE-TO-EARNINGS RATIO (P/E)

What Is the Price-to-Earnings Ratio?

This ratio is used by investors to evaluate whether a stock is overpriced or underpriced—and to project future earnings. It's the current price of the stock divided by its earnings the previous year.

How Do I Calculate the Price-to-Earnings Ratio?

You divide the current price of the stock by its annual per-share reported earnings.
If a $50 stock had per-share earnings of $2 last year, it has a P/E ratio of 25, which is considered historically to be on the high side. (For more information on P/E ratios and growth stocks, see Chapter 17.)

What Does Price-to-Earnings Mean to Me?

Price-to-earnings is really a way to compare similar types of companies. Pretend you're

---

WHEN LOSERS ARE WINNERS
The Internet revolution has created a whole new category of stocks: shares of companies that have never made a profit. One way to measure these companies is by loss per share (LPS). The tremendous capital investment needed to compete online in a global economy means many new technology businesses haven't made any money—they're pouring all their revenue into the business, for now. See Chapter 17 for thoughts on how to assess these companies.

Q. WHY IS AN OVERPRICED STOCK LIKE AN OVERPRICED DRESS?
A: BECAUSE YOU PROBABLY THINK THEY'RE BOTH A BAD DEAL.
Exactly. Generally speaking, if a stock's underpriced, it may have more room for greater earnings growth. An overpriced stock may have less room and could be more vulnerable in the event of a market decline. Although some people believe it's more difficult to make money (and thus riskier) owning an overpriced stock, it's not impossible. Think about *Titanic* (the movie, not the ship). With astronomical production costs of $200 million, plus another $200 million in advertising expenses, look what the movie had to rake in to turn even a modest profit. Well, its profits were more than modest, with more than $1 billion in worldwide revenues (and still going).

bent on buying stock in one of two toy companies. Gizmo Corporation has a P/E ratio of 15, and Toys for Joys has a P/E ratio of 12. Assuming both companies are pretty similar on other dimensions, you would be inclined to view Toys for Joys as less expensive due to its lower P/E and Gizmo Corporation as more expensive, with a higher P/E.

6. Track the Stock's Performance Online. When making a buy-sell decision, experienced investors not only research a stock's here-and-now pricing information and trading history but look at how it's performed over the previous weeks, months, even years. As an online investor, you can do this, too, by calling, and customizing, historical and intraday charts of individual stocks or combinations of stocks. These charts enable you to review a stock's performance, as well as to compare its performance with other stocks in the same industry or market index, over whatever time period and frequency (day, week, month, year) you choose to cover.

Can I read your chart?
Whether it spans a day, a month, six months, a year, five years, or longer, most stock performance charts actually consist of two charts. The top chart plots the stock's price movements and indicators (up or down earnings, dividends and splits) during that period; the bottom chart plots the volume up or down of shares in the millions traded that period.

Historical Chart (One Year)

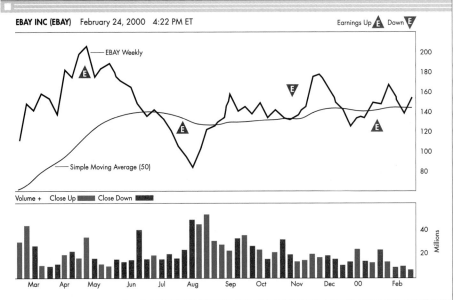

EBAY INC (EBAY) February 24, 2000 4:22 PM ET   Earnings Up ▲ Down ▼

EBAY Weekly
Simple Moving Average (50)

Volume +   Close Up   Close Down

Mar Apr May Jun Jul Aug Sep Oct Nov Dec 00 Feb

Though past performance is no guarantee of future results, many traders use charts to spot patterns that may indicate what a particular stock, segment, or the market as a whole might do. A historical chart allows you to track changes in price and volume; follow the moving averages; and note dividends, earnings, and stock splits from a single day to a decade ago. With an intraday chart you can track price and volume movements at five-minute intervals throughout the current trading day. As you become more experienced, you may want to create your own charts, adding your own combinations of more advanced indicator tools (such as MACD, Stochastic and Bollinger Bands—all of which I'll explain in Chapter 18) to track price performance and spot potential trends with the sophisticated eye of an experienced analyst.

7. Assess Risk and Reward Online. Looking at a company's profile and financial information is a fundamental tool for

---

Company Snapshot

EBAY INC (EBAY)   Updated 1/29/00   Data Source: Market Guide Inc.

Performance   Financials   Key Ratios   Dividends & Splits

Industry: Business Services

Key Ratios & Statistics

Price & Volume		Valuation Ratios	
Recent Price $	147.56	Price/Earnings (TTM)	2,588.83
52 Week High $	234.00	Price/Sales (TTM)	113.96
52 Week Low $	64.00	Price/Book (MRQ)	23.08
Avg Daily Vol (Mil)	3.58	Price/Cash Flow (TTM)	873.15
Beta	NA	**Per Share Data**	
Share Related Items		Earnings (TTM) $	0.06
Mkt. Cap. (Mil) $	19,085.65	Sales (TTM) $	1.30
Shares Out (Mil)	129.34	Book Value (MRQ) $	6.39
Float (Mil)	34.90	Cash Flow (TTM) $	0.17
Dividend Information		Cash (MRQ) $	2.99
Yield %	0.00	**Mgmt Effectiveness**	
Annual Dividend	0.00	Return on Equity (TTM)	1.92
Payout Ratio (TTM) %	0.00	Return on Assets (TTM)	1.71
Financial Strength		Return on Investment (TTM)	1.88
Quick Ratio (MRQ)	5.71	**Profitability**	
Current Ratio (MRQ)	6.07	Gross Margin (TTM) %	77.09
LT Debt/Equity (MRQ)	0.01	Operating Margin (TTM) %	0.27
Total Debt/Equity (MRQ)	0.02	Profit Margin (TTM) %	4.38

Mil = Millions   MRQ = Most Recent Quarter   TTM = Trailing Twelve Months

Price Performance

Period	Actual (%)	vs. S&P 500 (%)	Rank in Industry	Industry Rank
4 Week	17.9	27.3	73	87
13 Week	9.2	9.5	44	87
26 Week	51.1	47.6	78	89
52 Week	59.5	50.1	81	67
YTD	17.9	27.3	73	87

Note: Rank is a Percentile that Ranges from 0 to 99, with 99 = Best

Institutional Ownership		Insider Trading (Prev. 6 months)	
% Shares Owned	17.30	Net Insider Trades	−25
# of Institutions	267	# Buy Transactions	0
Total Shares Held (Mil)	22.373	# Sell Transactions	25
3 Mo. Net Purchases (Mil)	3.494	Net Shares Purchased (Mil)	−2.830
3 Mo. Shares Purchased (Mil)	7.614	# Shares Purchased (Mil)	0.000
3 Mo. Shares Sold (Mil)	4.120	# Shares Sold (Mil)	2.830

Source: Vickers Institutional Research

Short Interest

deciding whether a stock meshes with your personal and financial goals and objectives. You'll also find valuable data for calculating how much risk you may be taking by investing in that security relative to the reward you want to receive.

8. Check Out the Company's Web Site. Virtually every publicly held company has a Web site. Go there—you'll be amazed at the amount of information they want you to have, including such things as recent news, new products information, their annual report, and their filings with the SEC. As you grow experienced in reading financial statements, you can often tell at a glance what the company's situation really is.

9. Research Market Analyst Projections Online. Online information gives you the power to be your own stock analyst. But why not get a second (or third) opinion? The appraisals of professional market watchers who track the equities markets for a living often impact that market with their projections. Their analyses can be a useful supplement to your own efforts in sizing up a particular stock, group of stocks, or market sector. E*TRADE provides consensus earnings, revenue and dividend estimates, as well as projected growth rates and ratios, on thousands of stocks for the most recent quarter all the way back to five years ago from the country's leading brokerages to help you make your judgment call.

BUY, SELL, DUCK, AND COVER

There is rarely 100 percent agreement on anything—and the securities markets are no exception. You can find analysts who agree with you on virtually any position you want to take. Think a stock will go down? Someone agrees with you. Think it'll go up? Someone else agrees with you. In a curious way, this disagreement can actually be a comfort to you. Whatever decision (or investment strategy) you choose, someone else out there has come to the same conclusion you have—oftentimes for the same reasons. Neither one of you may be right, but at least you agree.

10. Insider Trading and Institutional Ownership. Information in these areas can provide you with valuable clues. Company insiders, defined as officers, directors, or anyone owning more than 5 percent of a company, are required by law to disclose the purchase or sale of their own company's stock. Selling might indicate they feel the stock has peaked (or they may simply have a kid headed to

Harvard). Some insiders sell on a regular schedule to minimize speculation. Buying could mean they think the stock's undervalued. In addition, you can research the number of shares owned by institutions such as pension funds and mutual fund companies. Often, the people who handle these investments are seasoned pros and their trades can reveal what sophisticated investors think of the stock.

News

EBAY INC (EBAY)

01/31/2000 17:25 •	Amazon, eBay used as models for LatAm newcomers – *Reuters*
01/31/2000 16:26 •	Feds keep Nets on edge – *CBS MarketWatch*
01/31/2000 09:00 •	Tangible Asset Galleries, Inc. Now Fully Compliant With NASD R – *Business Wire*
01/31/2000 08:41 •	Sales OnLine Direct and News Alert Sign Agreement to Offer Vis – *Business Wire*
01/31/2000 08:14 •	BullTrade.com Announces Investment Opinion; BullTrade.com Spec – *Business Wire*
01/29/2000 17:03 •	Venture capital forum honors women CEOs – *CBS MarketWatch*
01/28/2000 19:17 •	Nets brace for higher interest rates – *CBS MarketWatch*
01/28/2000 19:16 •	SmartPortfolio.Com Announces Investment Opinion – *Business Wire*
01/27/2000 09:02 •	Shares prepare for higher open – *CBS MarketWatch*
01/26/2000 12:46 •	Tech stocks soften as Qualcomm slips – *CBS MarketWatch*

MORE STORIES ▶

11. Scan the News. The morning paper and the evening news are filled with items of interest to investors. Not only are the doings of major companies (especially in the high-tech arena) often front-page news, but news that seemingly has nothing whatsoever to do with your portfolio (A cold snap in the farm belt? War in an oil-rich nation?) can sometimes affect your share prices.

12. Keep Up with Market News Online. We live in a global economy. Virtually every major corporation does business globally and generally has some kind of presence overseas as well. Changes in foreign economies and foreign markets often have an impact on the sales and earnings of domestic companies. The best way to know what's going on is to read. Do the research—it's right there for you. A good financial service provider will allow you to catch up on:

- Breaking company news and market analyses.
- Coverage of premarket, market day and extended-hours market conditions with expert commentary. Real-time

analyst upgrades and downgrades, company press releases about new product and service offerings, business ventures, financial reports, and stock issues and splits.

And, of course, a good financial service provider will provide you with the tools to monitor the markets 24 hours a day, seven days a week, 365 days a year (366 in leap years).

ARE COMMUNITY MESSAGE BOARDS AND CHAT ROOMS SAFE?

Safe from whom? If you're uninformed and believe you should act on every tidbit you pick up, then they're not a place to linger. But we believe you have the right to govern yourself and make your own decisions about what you see and hear. Through E*TRADE's online community, we give you that freedom which should be coupled with a healthy skepticism. But to ensure a quality environment we keep an eye on the neighborhood ourselves. If we see something that might imply insider information, possible stock manipulation or otherwise violate stated community policies, it's pulled, and we report insider information or stock manipulation to the regulators.

13. Join the Online Community. Company focused discussion groups, chat forums, financial clubs, specialized investment discussions (beer budget, value investing, growth investing), live Q&A. Within the E*TRADE community you can find dozens of ways you can connect with investors like yourself and investors who are nothing like you. Forming relationships and associations can help you share viewpoints and ideas in the ever-expanding digital universe of shared knowledge. The online community is fast becoming one of the key resources of information that self-directed investors want. It's a digital hub that allows you to communicate with others of like mind with similar investment styles, goals, and experiences, sharing multiple points of view that add another dimension to your own decision-making.

14. Create a Watch List. One way to find your risk comfort level—and to find out who's got good (and bad) advice on the Internet—is to create a watch list, a portfolio of stocks you don't own but are simply "watching." Join a discussion group. Listen to what they're saying. Consider their ideas. Enter the security (and the day and date you could have "bought" it) into a newly created fantasy portfolio. Over the weeks and months, track the performance of these "test" buys and see how well (or how poorly) you would have done listening to someone else's advice.

"Thanks for the tips, Christos, but what do I do with all that information?"

Let's go back to your target number—and back to the legal disclaimer in the front of the book. Remember the lawyers' statement? "Past performance is no guarantee of future returns." Research is your tool to make an evaluation without having to rely solely on past performance.

Say your target number is 18 percent. You do some research and you see that Growfast, Inc.'s stock has been growing fast—averaging about 18 percent a year. At first glance, you think "hmmm, this stock would be right for my portfolio." But your research starts to tell you a different story. In scanning the news, you read that all of Growfast's competitors have updated their manufacturing facilities, but Growfast hasn't. It looks like Growfast will have to make a huge capital investment in their plants over the next few years—or risk losing market share. Suddenly, Growfast isn't looking like a good bet to continue its 18 percent growth!

Research is your personal tool to make as good an evaluation as possible as to whether a company can match your investment goals.

> **ARE YOU GAME?**
>
> If you're new to investing, you might want to try all this out on the E*TRADE Game first. It's free and you don't even have to have an account to play. On top of that, we give you $100,000 (in play money, of course) to get started. It's a great way to take the pressure off while you learn the process of investing online.

Placing a Stock Order Online

Ready to place an order?

You did your research. You like the company, its product, its history, and its performance. You think it's a winner. It's time to place your order.

(To show you the process, I'll be using E*TRADE's methods. If you're not investing with us, many of these steps, with some navigational modifications, can be followed at the sites of other online financial service providers.)

Step 1. Using your mouse, go to the Trading area, which is where all the action takes place. Then select Enter Order under the Stocks heading.

Step 2. Select the transaction type. In this example, let's select Buy. (We'll talk about Sell, Sell Short and Buy to Cover later.)

Step 3. Enter the number of shares for this order. Stocks usually trade in 100 share increments known as round lots, so you may want to make things easier by placing your order in multiples of 100. If you want to buy only 10 shares (or 53 or 174), however, you can do that, too; it's called an *odd lot*.

Enter Stock Order

Account Number: 8889-2212   **Switch Accounts**

Transaction:	Number of Shares:	Stock Symbol:	Price:
● Buy			● Market
○ Sell	100	EBAY	○ Limit
○ Sell Short			○ Stop:
○ Buy to Cover			○ Stop Limit:

Term:

Good for Day ▼   **Optional:** ○ All-or-None (If 300+ shares)

Trading Password: ★ ★ ★ ★ ★ ★   **PREVIEW ORDER**   **CLEAR**

Step 4. Enter the stock symbol, or if you don't know the symbol click Find Symbol for help identifying it. (But you should already know the symbol because you've been researching and tracking the stock, right?)

Step 5. Select the type of order you'd like to place, providing specific information, if necessary. You have four choices:

- **Market.** A market order means just what it says. You place the order, it is sent to the market (during market hours), and whatever the going ask price is (for a buy order) when the order is received by the market, you'll get it. It could be what you see in a quote, or it could change. When you place a market order, you're saying, "Buy or sell the shares for me at the going rate!"

- **Limit.** A limit order is a bit different. When you place a limit order, you're saying "This is the most I want to pay" or "I want to get at least this much when I sell." You're naming your specific price, not giving in to the whims of the market. Does this mean you'll buy or sell the shares? Not necessarily. With a buy order, if the ask price is above your limit price, your order won't fill. And it's the same way if you are selling: If the bid is below your limit price, your order will sit there and wait to be filled. Your order will also sit and wait if there are significant "shares ahead" of your limit order at the same price and not enough quantity to fill all the limit orders at that price.

For a buy order, you really don't need to worry about Stop or Stop Limit. We'll cover those when we talk about selling.

Step 6. Select the time period for your order, Good for Day or Good-Until-Canceled (GTC) Order. What's the difference? A Day order is good for today. That's it. If the order doesn't fill by the close of market, forget about it. A Good-Until-Canceled order says, "Keep on trying. Tomorrow's another day." Your order stays open until it fills, you change it, or, at E*TRADE, 60 days go by (at which point, enough is enough, and the order gets canceled). Market orders can be placed only as Good for Day orders.

Step 7. For orders over 300 shares, you can also tell the market that you want to buy a very specific number of shares, and if you can't, you're just not interested. That's

> **STAY ALERT!**
> When you place a buy or sell order for a stock, you can also program your account to alert you when the stock moves in any direction you set. At E*TRADE just click Alerts and enter the criteria you want. The system will alert you (either in your account or directly to your e-mail address) when the selected stock hits the criteria you specify.

called an all-or-none (AON) order. If this is what you want, click the checkbox beside All or None. With this type of order, if the exact number of shares you want is not available, the trade will not be executed. Be aware that an AON order has a qualifier, which means it might lead to manual processing and slow down your order.

Step 8. Enter your trading password and click Preview Order. At E*TRADE the Preview Order page includes a real-time quote so you can compare the price you're willing to pay for a stock with its actual trading price. Review the symbol, transaction type, price, quantity and total value of the order.

Preview Stock Order

January 31, 2000 3:50 PM ET

EBAY INC — Real-time quote

Symbol	Price	Change	Bid	Ask	Volume
EBAY	150	$2^9{}_{16}$	150	$150^1{}_{16}$	2,035,500

Sally Friedman 8889-2212: **Margin Account**

Your Order

Transaction	Quantity	Symbol & Company Name	Your Price	Term
Buy	100	EBAY – EBAY INC	Mkt	Day

Current Ask	Time	Est. Commision	Est. Total Order
$150^1{}_{16}$	03:50 PM	19.95	15,026.20

IMPORTANT: You are placing a firm order. Please review carefully.
Note: Click only once to place your order.

PLACE ORDER   **CANCEL ORDER**

Step 9. If everything's okay (be sure to check the information carefully) and you want to go ahead, click the Place Order button and—Presto!— off the order goes. You've placed the order. You're on your way. You've done it. You've joined the online investing revolution!

Confirmation

Account: 8889-2212

Your stock order was placed at 3:51 PM ET 01/31/00.

This transaction is order number **155**.

"Okay, Christos, you've shown me how to buy. But when should I sell?"

Stock prices can fluctuate greatly over the short term. Changes in the market, in economic factors, in a particular sector and within a particular company can affect stock prices both short and long term. Market timing is very difficult to predict. Stay focused. Keep an eye on the markets, your investments, and your target number to determine when you should consider selling.

How do you make money in the stock market? Ideally you buy low and sell high. But if you sell all your investments when they're losing money and buy investments that are at or near all-time highs, then you're practically guaranteed to lose money in the stock market.

> **WHAT IF I'M NOT HOME?**
>
> On vacation with no access to a computer? At E*TRADE you can still connect to your account and place an order. Our 24-hour touch-tone or speech recognition telephone investing system (called TELE*MASTER®) gives you complete access to your account and the ability to place orders anytime, from anywhere.

When Stocks Move Up

You gleefully rub your hands and count your paper (unrealized) profits. But that's all they are: *paper profits*. At some point, you've got to take them to make them. So what do you do when that highflying stock that you expected to go up 20 percent in a year actually goes up 40 percent? It depends on the investment, on the market, on your target number and your goals.

Is the stock's fantastic rate of growth sustainable? Is it outperforming its sector? Why? If the company controls a large portion of its market, where's new growth going to come from? Unless the market itself is growing, the company may not have anywhere to go. Watch the stock in relation to your target number and do your research to determine if the stock is going to continue to meet your goals or if you might be better off locking in that gain and moving your money to an investment that's more on target.

When Stocks Go Down

Find out why. *And don't just settle for the official version the company puts out.* Again, do your research. Is the entire market moving down as well? Then chances are your investment will rebound when the market does. Is the entire industry moving down? Then compare your investment to the industry as a whole. Is your stock outperforming its industry? If it is, and the reasons the industry's in recession are understandable and temporary, you might want to actually buy more shares of the company. That way, you'd be dollar-cost-averaged in at a lower price than you originally paid—and you'll be poised to reap larger profits in any rebound.

But what if you picked a loser? It happens. The hard part is determining whether you've picked a real dog with no hope of recovery or you're actually holding another Chrysler. There's often not a clear answer, and it will come down to your investment temperament: Can you ride it out all the way—possibly losing even more money—or do you want to cut your losses and run? It's a tough call. No matter which one you choose, remember there are thousands of new opportunities, good and bad, out there every day.

A Time to Sell

When you're ready to sell shares of a stock held in your account, you can place your sell order online, similar to the way we placed a buy order. You can sell all or just a portion of the shares you hold. Once the sale has cleared, proceeds from the transaction will automatically be credited to your account.

When placing a sell order, you have a number of choices for specifying the selling price. You can enter a market order and take whatever the going bid price is for the stock at the time your order reaches the market. You can enter a limit order and specify the minimum price you'd like to sell the shares for. You can also enter a stop order (also known as stop-loss) and specify a "trigger" price for creating a market order.

With a stop order, you're saying "Sell this stock as soon as it has traded at this price." If (and when) that time comes, your trade will be executed just like a market order. A stop order is a trip wire. If the stock is trading at 50 and you want to make sure you sell the stock if it tanks to 40, you place a stop order at 40. If the stock then falls to that price, your order turns into a market order and the shares sell at the next available bid price. This price could be near the stop price or not—to ensure more control over the actual trading price, you'll need to enter a stop limit order.

With a stop limit order, your order becomes a limit order if and when the stop price is reached. Your shares are triggered for sale at the stop price, but can actually only sell when the limit price is reached. A stop order can guarantee your shares will trade if the stop price is reached but it can't guarantee the price they'll trade at. A stop limit order guarantees the price, but not necessarily that the shares are going to trade (because the limit price may not be met). Got it?

Selling Short

Did you know you could sell high, buy low and still make money? It's done through a technique called selling short. This potentially risky strategy involves selling shares of a stock that you don't own. Your financial service provider "borrows" them for you with the expectation that you'll be able to buy the shares back later at a cheaper price and **cover** your position. Because the risks associated with short selling involve more than just your initial investment, this technique is only for the experienced investor with nerves of steel.

buy to cover
Buying stock to close a short position. The opposite of selling short.

Online Bond Investing

Take a break, you've earned it. We've already covered a lot of information and there's lots more to learn. Just don't get discouraged. This is important stuff. This is for your financial future.

What You Can Do Online

- **Get** current price information on fixed-income securities trading on the North American OTC market.
- **Search** for bonds that meet your specific investment needs and objectives.
- **Research** quality ratings on many thousands of issues.
- **Compare** projected returns between bonds.
- **Know** what's going on in the enormous bond market —what's new, what's hot, and what's not.

Here's how.

Search for Bonds Online

Literally millions of issues are available—and more bonds are auctioned every day. Unless you're interested in a specific bond, and know its exact ID number, you'll have to look around for one that will work for you. The search for bonds that match your investment needs is similar to the search for mutual funds: You've got to define your criteria and do a search with some kind of search engine. Although other financial service providers may have some kind of bond search mechanism, this is one of those examples where I have to say that E*TRADE's Bond Center has the most sophisticated bond searching and investing tools on the Web. Although I use our Bond Center as an example, you probably won't currently find anything like it at any other financial service provider.

At the E*TRADE Bond Center, you can find fixed-income securities by category:

- U.S. treasuries (bonds, bills, notes, strips)
- Investment and non-investment grade corporate bonds
- Municipal bonds
- Federal agency bonds

And, you can search through each category to find:

- New bond offerings available for immediate execution (purchase)
- Outstanding bonds and "live" offerings that have been on the market and are currently available

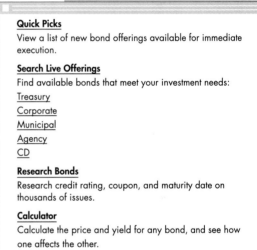

Inside the Bond Center

Quick Picks
View a list of new bond offerings available for immediate execution.

Search Live Offerings
Find available bonds that meet your investment needs:
Treasury
Corporate
Municipal
Agency
CD

Research Bonds
Research credit rating, coupon, and maturity date on thousands of issues.

Calculator
Calculate the price and yield for any bond, and see how one affects the other.

▼ Buy Bonds

Enter the search criteria you care most about to find all bonds in each category that match or come close to your investing requirements. If the highest rating matters to you, make that your principal selection. If maturity is important, select that. You can sort bonds by:

- **Issue.** Bonds of a particular issuer.
- **CUSIP.** Bonds by ID number.
- **Maturity.** Bonds due and payable within the time frame you desire.
- **Coupon.** Bonds paying the annual rate of interest you want.
- **Price.** Bonds for the highest or lowest prices you're willing to go.
- **Rating.** Rated bonds, or all bonds with a specific rating (see Assessing Risk and Reward following).

Size Up Bonds Online

Your category search produces a focus list of new or outstanding bonds that meet your criteria. You can move directly to placing your buy/sell order, or if you want more information in order to make a decision, link to a more detailed quote on that offering.

Reading a Detailed Bond Quote Online

Data	What It Tells You
S&P/Moody grade	The bond's investment quality as rated by the two major bond grading services.
frequency	How often interest is paid on the bond.
settlement	The date when you must pay for the bond (or payment must be made to you) and the bonds are delivered to, or removed from, your account.
first coupon	The date when the first interest payment for the bond will be made.
last coupon	The date when the last interest payment for the bond was made.
bid price	The price you could sell the bond for.
offer price	The price you could buy the bond for.
yield to maturity	The real rate of return on the bond, taking into account its coupon, time to maturity, and dollar price.
current yield	For new issues, the annual rate of interest the bond issuer pays the bond holder until maturity. Otherwise, it's annual income divided by current market price.

quantity	The maximum number of bonds available at that price.
duration	A measure of the bond's exposure to interest rate risk until maturity.
call date	The earliest that a callable bond may be redeemed by the issuer.
call price	The total amount the issuer must pay the holder for a callable bond redeemed early.

Assessing Risk and Reward

In the world of bonds, ratings and quality go hand in hand. In Chapter 8 we discussed the letter ratings given by Standard & Poor's and Moody's—the two independent services that assign each bond a rating keyed to the financial strength and debt-paying reliability of the issuer. The higher a bond's rating, the lower the risk.

Remember to check the bond's ratings as part of your research. And remember that Treasury bonds aren't rated—because they're the people who print the money.

Calculate Returns

Estimate the reward you expect to receive for the price you'll be paying for the bond, and how price affects yield. E∗TRADE's Bond Calculator lets you run the numbers online. Just check the Price and Yield fields, then enter the bond's characteristics which can be found in the detailed description of the offering on the labeled screens. The figures you come up with, which show you the estimated yield to maturity you can expect on the bond relative to price, should be viewed as a modeling exercise and not a recommendation of a particular investment. Use it as one more search tool to help you to make up your own mind.

CALLING ALL BONDS! CALLING ALL BONDS!

If interest rates drop, companies that issue bonds can save a lot of money by paying off existing debt and floating new bonds at a more advantageous (to them) lower rate. That's why many long-term corporate and municipal bonds include a call provision, giving them the contractual right to pay their bonds off before maturity, usually for a premium paid to the holder.

ALL GOVERNMENTS ARE NOT CREATED EQUAL

Although Treasury bonds are considered safe and aren't rated, that's not true of governments other than the federal government and other types of government agencies. From time to time we hear about different cities or different regional authorities that threaten to default on their debt. If you're researching municipal bonds, don't forget to check the rating!

WHY BUY BONDS?

If bonds have risks and their price varies, why should you buy bonds in the first place? To diversify your portfolio. You don't just want different stocks or different bonds or different mutual funds, you want different *categories of securities*. That way, if the stock market moves down, oftentimes that's offset by an upward movement in bonds.

Open a Window on the Bond Markets

Are prices trending higher or lower for shorter versus longer term treasuries? Are new issues of investment-grade corporate bonds from well-heeled companies on the rise or slowing down? Is the demand for municipals trending stronger or weaker?

Are political uncertainties in overseas government bond markets presenting specific buying opportunities you should look out for or avoid?

The answers to these questions, and the supporting data behind those answers, may help you with your decision-making. Or they may even refocus your search on a different category of bonds or bond market altogether.

You can get these answers, and more, by reading whatever bond market news and analysis is offered by your online broker. For example, the "Commentary" page at E*TRADE's Bond Center links you to summaries and breakdowns of what's happening and why, in the U.S. Treasury, corporate, municipal, agency as well as rated European, Asian, and Latin American government bond markets, provided weekly by the *Financial Times* and Interactive Data.

BUYING BONDS ON MARGIN

Like stocks (but unlike mutual funds), you can buy bonds on margin—provided their S&P/Moody's rating is A or better and they're trading at or above 70 percent of par value. Is this a good idea? It's up to you. Just remember one of the fundamental investment strategies: Pay off your debt!

Placing a Bond Order Online

A few financial service providers make it easy to buy and sell bonds by including a wide variety of bonds in their bond trading section. At E*TRADE's Bond Center, for example, you can invest in Treasuries, corporates, municipals, agencies, zeros, and CDs. Here's how:

Step 1. Go to the Trading area and select Bonds.

Step 2. To buy bonds, click Buy Bonds. To sell bonds, click Sell Bonds. You have some additional options:

- **Bid Wanted.** If you are selling, you can use Bid Wanted to solicit the highest price the market is willing to pay to buy a particular bond from you. (It may take 15 minutes or so to get a response.)
- **Offer Wanted.** If you are buying, you can use Offer Wanted to solicit the lowest price at which the market is currently willing to sell you a particular bond.
- **Quote Request.** Use this to ask for available bids and offers on a specific bond. (It may take 15 minutes or so to get a response.)
- **Treasury Auction.** Choose this if you wish to buy treasuries at auction.

Step 3. At Number of Bonds, type the number of bonds that you want to buy or sell. Some bond dealers require minimums. You will be notified of this when you Preview your order.

Step 4. At Bond CUSIP, type the bond's ID number. If you don't know the CUSIP, you can search E*TRADE's current bond offerings and get the number. Click Search Current Offerings and select the type of bond that you want.

Enter Bond Order

Account Number: 8889-2212 **? HELP**

Issue: United States Treas Bds callable 05/09@100

Product Type: Treasury **Coupon:** 13.25 **Maturity:** 05/15/2014

Transaction:	Number of Bonds:	Bond CUSIP:
Buy	10	912810DJ4

Quantity Offer Pricing (based on settlement 01/31/2000)

Qty:	1–24	25–49	50–74	75–99	100+
Price:	143.301	143.270	143.238	143.223	143.207
YTM:	8.083	8.086	8.089	8.090	8.092
YTC:	6.867	6.871	6.875	6.877	6.878

Trading Password: ★ ★ ★ ★ ★ ★   **PREVIEW ORDER**   **CLEAR**

Step 5. At Pricing choose:

- **Market.** Buy or sell the bond at its best price.
- **Price.** This lets you buy or sell the bond at a price you specify. Careful! The price is specified per $100. For example, if you enter $95.50 you are buying $1,000 of face value for $955.
- **Yield.** This lets you buy or sell a bond at a specific yield, rather than a specific price. Yield, as you may recall, is the basis on which a bond is priced and sold. It reflects the value of the bond giving consideration to the length of time to maturity, credit quality of the issuer/guarantor, and general market conditions.

Step 6. Enter your trading password, then click Preview Order.

Preview Bond Order

Account: 8889-2212   January 27, 2000 4:29 PM ET

Transaction	Execution Type	Face Value($)	CUSIP	Product Type
Buy	Firm	$10,000.00	912810DJ4	Treasury

Issue	Coupon	Maturity	Coupons Per Year	Trade Type
United States Treasury Bds Callable 5/09@100	13.25	05/15/2014	2	Principal

Qty	Price	Yield	Principal	Settlement	Accrued Interest	Transfer Fee	Est. Total Order
10	143.7008	8.045	$14,370.08	01/31/2000	$280.29 (77 days)	$40.00	$14,650.37

IMPORTANT:
Please review carefully. You are placing a firm order.

PLACE ORDER   **CANCEL**

Step 7. Check your order carefully to ensure that you've entered everything correctly. If you would like to change your order, you must do it at this point. To change the order, click Cancel Order and start over. Otherwise, click Place Order.

CHAPTER 14

Online Mutual Fund Investing

M utual funds are extremely popular. You should already know why: They offer the ability to invest in a lot of different companies just by investing in a single mutual fund. And those various investments (the fund's portfolio) are managed by a professional money manager. Moreover, when the holdings in a mutual fund change, as they often do, sometimes daily, the various portfolio transactions are seamless to a mutual fund shareholder.

So what's the catch? Like any investment, a mutual fund needs to be thoroughly researched. At a minimum, you should understand the fund's objective, how the fund's portfolio is invested, the historical performance of the fund *and* the fund manager, and the types of commissions or loads the fund charges.

It's a Big Number
In 1999, mutual fund assets increased 24 percent to $6.843 trillion.

What You Can Do Online

- **Select** funds by fund family, fee type, objective, or investment strategy.
- **Search** for funds that meet your specific criteria: investment objective, historical performance, portfolio

management strategy, and more.

- **Get** a current quote on a particular mutual fund.
- **Track** a fund's performance over the past year, or years.
- **View** a breakdown of the assets in a specific fund portfolio.
- **Read** a fund's prospectus online, or print it out to review later at your leisure.
- **Chat** with some of today's leading fund managers and asset management professionals for insight into the growing and evolving mutual fund market.
- **Buy**, **sell**, or **exchange** mutual funds.

Online mutual fund investing gives you the power to do all these things. Some financial service providers have screening filters and analysis tools to help you weigh your choices among mutual fund offerings and make selections keyed to your individual requirements and the specific objective of your personal financial plan—your target number.

Finding the Funds for You

You can start your search by listing all funds from A to Z, and call them up one by one for closer scrutiny. This is a dreadful strategy unless you've got nothing better to do every night for a year or so, in which case it's probably better for you than watching TV.

At the E*TRADE Mutual Fund Center, you can search through categories of funds such as no-load funds, no-fee funds or you can use the Power Search and focus in on more detailed criteria.

Select Power Search and you'll see a broad range of criteria (and multiple choices within them) to help focus your search. For example, under Investment Objective, you'll find 36 different categories—from aggressive growth funds to world funds. Power Search criteria work together to generate a list of mutual funds that have all, not just one, of the characteristics you're looking for. You don't have to specify every criteria offered, but the fewer you specify, the bigger the list you'll generate. Experiment. Repeat the search process as often as you like, using as many new or different combinations of criteria as you want. Some criteria you'll find include:

Fund Family. Find all the funds offered by a particular management company, for example E*TRADE Asset Management, Inc., Janus, American Century, Invesco, etc.

Investment Objective. Find funds that match an objective of your personal financial plan, such as growth and income, aggressive growth, asset allocation, balanced portfolio, and so on.

Historical Performance. Find funds that had returns over a given period at or above a certain percentage.

Fund Assets. Find funds based on value of assets (dollar amount of assets in stocks, bonds, and cash equivalents).

Age of Fund. Find funds according to the minimum or maximum length of time they've been on the market.

Minimum Initial Investment. Find funds according to the minimum amount you'd have to invest to buy into them. For many investors, this is an important heads-up because funds generally also set minimums for future investments (often different than the initial investment).

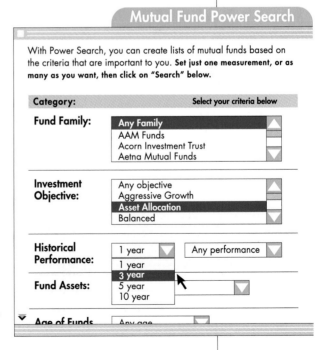

loads
Additional fees added by certain mutual funds to the purchase and/or sale price of the fund. Mutual funds are often categorized by how they charge these fees.

Commission Type. Find funds according to **loads** charged for purchasing or selling the fund in addition to (or instead of) transaction fees.

Operating Expense Ratio. Find funds whose overhead costs, management, advisory, and other expenses don't exceed a certain percentage of the fund's assets, for example, a fund whose expenses are 3 percent of the fund's assets or lower.

12b-1 Fee. Find funds whose annual charges are no more than a certain percentage of the fund's average assets.

Qualified In. Find funds that can be bought and sold in a particular state, or any state.

Portfolio Management Strategy. Find funds that invest in a specific asset class (for example, bond funds); in a particular geographic region, such as emerging market funds in Asia or Latin America; a particular market sector, such as high-tech company stocks and bonds; or market index, such as the Dow Jones Industrial Average or S&P 500.

LOAD 'EM UP!

In case you don't remember from our discussion about mutual funds in Chapter 9, different funds have different ways of charging commissions.

front-end load
A sales charge for purchasing shares.

back-end load
A sales charge for placing a sell order; the percentage depends upon how long you've held the shares.

level load
A percentage of the fund's average assets charged annually to cover the fund's advertising and marketing costs. Also called a 12b-1 fee.

no load
No sales charge (from the fund) for buying or selling shares.

Annual Portfolio Turnover. Find funds whose rate of buying or selling securities each year is no higher than a certain percentage; many investors use this criterion because of the tax ramifications a high turnover rate may present.

Fund Manager Tenure. Find funds based on the number of years the current fund manager has been managing a particular fund.

Hold on just a minute.

As you read through this list, you might be saying to yourself, "Gee, Christos, mutual fund investing is a bit more complicated than I thought." Well, just like other forms of investing, in the initial phases of mutual fund investing, there's a lot to learn. And a lot of your research will include learning what many new terms mean and what significance these features might have in relation to a particular mutual fund you may be interested in.

Again, to quickly identify a list of funds that meet your specific criteria online, you don't need to designate a choice for every option. But the more you know and the more criteria you specify, the quicker you'll be able to hone in on the funds that are right for you.

Risk Measures. Find funds according to their levels of risk (volatility), as measured by past performance. Select the risk quantifiers you're most interested in, or all four:

1. **Alpha.** Find funds whose past returns exceeded expectations (positive alpha) in a given period, or who didn't fall below a certain negative alpha over the same period in projected versus actual returns.

2. **Beta.** Find funds that showed the same volatility (positive beta) in a given period as its benchmark index, or no more than a certain level of volatility (negative beta) than its benchmark index over the same period.

3. **Sharpe Ratio.** Find funds whose risk-adjusted returns in a given period exceeded those of lower risk investments, such as U.S. Treasury bills.

4. **R-Squared.** Find funds whose fluctuation in value over a given period was equal to or no greater than the fluctuation in value of its benchmark index over the same period.

Sizing Up Mutual Funds Online

Once you've narrowed your search, link to each underlined fund to pull up a quote and access other research information to make your analysis and determine which fund may be right for you.

Reading a Mutual Fund Quote Online

Data	What It Tells You
net asset value (NAV)	The current (as of the previous day) dollar value per share of the fund, less any loads or other fees.
day change	Percent change, plus or minus, in the fund's NAV from the previous market close.
public offer price (POP)	Current cost per share, including loads or other fees, to buy into the fund.
previous close	Price per share at the end of the last trading session.
52 wk high/low	Percent gain or loss in the value of the fund over the past 12 months.

HOW'S YOUR NAV, POP?

Here's an easy way to tell if your fund is a no-load, front-end load, or back-end load: If the NAV is the same as the POP, it's a no-load fund. If the POP is higher than the NAV, it's a front-end load; if the NAV is higher than the POP, it's a back-end load. Easy, isn't it?

Mutual funds use what's called forward pricing. This means that the day's trading price isn't set until after market close. The price you see today is the price people paid for the fund shares yesterday. If you buy today, what you'll pay will depend on the price set by the fund after today's market close, so you won't know what you've actually paid until the next business day.

Assessing Risk and Reward

Mutual funds should be watched as carefully as any other investments. Because past performance is no guarantee of future results, thinking you've found the "perfect" fund might be true for a few months—but markets, managers, and investment opportunities change, and so does the performance of many funds. Buying a mutual fund without keeping an eye on its vital statistics may wind up costing you sleepless nights later on. E*TRADE's Mutual Fund Center provides a fund analysis page called Fund Facts where you can evaluate data on each fund's growth and return history, volatility characteristics, and other relevant details, as well as compare the potential risks/rewards of one fund against another. Information you can find includes:

- Growth in monthly returns over the past 10 years, or since the fund's inception, compared with the growth stats of its best index benchmark.

- Average annual total returns as of the end of the most recent quarter, year-to-date, over a 3, 5, or 10-year period, or since the fund's inception (whichever is shorter).

- Exact fees and minimums.

- Alpha, beta, Sharpe Ratio, and R-Squared volatility quantification.

- Detailed overviews of the fund's objective and manager's investment strategy.

- Portfolio composition broken down by percent invested in individual sectors (utilities, industrials, technologies, etc.); percent in each type of asset (stocks, bonds, foreign securities, cash); plus a list of its top 10 holdings.

> **TWINKLE, TWINKLE, LITTLE MORNINGSTAR**
>
> E•TRADE's Fund Facts are provided by Morningstar—a top independent resource for comprehensive research and analysis on thousands of mutual funds. You can find out more about them at www.morningstar.com.

Mutual Fund Quote

JANUS ENTERPRISE FUND (JAENX)
February 17, 2000 5:39 PM ET   Closing Prices

Net Asset Value: 92.19	**Day Change:** +2.77 (+3.10%)

Pub. Offer Price:	92.19	**Prev. Close:**	89.42
52 Wk High:	92.19 (2/17/2000)	**52 Wk Low:**	35.35 (2/17/1999)
Commission Type:	An E*TRADE no-load, no-transaction fee fund		

Reading the Fund's Prospectus

Each mutual fund prospectus provides a detailed description of the fund's goals, investing strategies, portfolio composition of investments and assets, fees, annual and quarterly reports of past performance history, as well as background on the fund's management team. All mutual fund companies are required by SEC regulation to make this comprehensive document available for free to mutual fund shoppers directly or through the shopper's broker.

You can read the prospectus of each mutual fund on your shopping list at E*TRADE's Mutual Fund Center, which makes the prospectuses of more than 5,000 funds available to online investors.

As a self-directed investor, you must read the prospectus of any fund in which you are considering an investment. This is essential if you are to complete your risk/reward analysis and have the fullest understanding of what you're getting into if you decide to buy a particular fund. We require that you indicate on our mutual funds order entry page that you have read the fund's prospectus before placing your buy order.

Remember, research with your target number in mind.

- What's the historic rate of return for a particular fund? Is it higher or lower than your number? Although past performance is no guarantee of future results, it's a good starting point.

- Who are the fund managers? Are they the same people who've been managing the fund in the past? What is their previous experience?

Fund Fact Sheet

JANUS ENTERPRISE FUND (JAENX)   As of 2/18/00   Data Source: Morningstar

Growth of $10,000   Last 10 Years vs. Wilshire 4500

■ Fund
— Wishire 4500 (Benchmark Index)

Average Annual Total Returns (%)

As of	YTD	1 Year	3 Year	5 Year	Since Inception
Quarter End	–	128.74%	50.23%	36.95%	
12/31/99	121.90%	121.90%	48.72%	36.12%	31.94%

General Information, including Fees and Minimums

	Initial	Subsequenet
Minimum Investment:	$2,500	$100
IRA Minimum Investment:	$500	$100

Fund Portfolio

		Top 10 Holdings
Utility	0.2%	Paychex
Energy	0 %	McLeodUSA Cl A
Financials	1.3%	Vitesse Semicon
Industrial Cyclicals	2.1%	Veritas Software
Consumer Durables	1.7%	SDL
Consumer Staples	0 %	Hispanic Brdcstg Cl A
Service	52.1%	Nextlink Comms Cl A
Retail	3.1%	Apollo Grp Cl A
Health	8.8%	Exodus Comms
Technology	30.8%	Metromedia Fiber Net Cl A

▾ Asset Breakdown

- What's the fund's strategy? Is it the same as yours? More aggressive? More conservative?
- Should you mix your funds? Just as you diversify stocks and bonds, you can also have more than one type of fund.
- Does the fund know something you know as well as you do? Do they invest in an industry you're familiar with? Are they making the same choices you'd make with those securities?

Buying Mutual Fund Shares Online

You've done your research. You've made as good a determination as you can that the fund you've selected can meet your investment needs. Now it's time to turn your research into an order.

(Again, the examples here are specific to E*TRADE, but other financial service providers that offer mutual fund investing may have similar procedures).

Step 1. Go to the Trading area, click Enter Order under the Mutual Funds heading. Select Buy a fund. At E*TRADE, you have three ways to identify which fund you'd like to invest in: If you know the fund's symbol, type it in at Enter the symbol of the fund, and click Buy This Fund. If you don't know the symbol, go to Choose from any of the funds available through E*TRADE, select a fund family, and click View members of the Fund Family. Then click Buy next to the fund you want.

Enter Mutual Fund Order

Step 1

Account Number: 8889-2212

Choose the fund you want to buy:

Enter the symbol of the Fund:

JAENX   **Buy This Fund**

–or–

Choose from any of the funds available through E*TRADE:

AIM Funds

View members of the Fund Family

Enter Mutual Fund Order

Step **2**

Account Number: 8889-2212

Complete your ordering information:
Fund Name: JANUS ENTERPRISE FUND
Fund Symbol: JAENX

Amount:

◉ Dollars $ [2,500]

○ Shares [   ]

○ Dollars, but no fractional shares $ [   ]

You're about to buy shares in a fund that you don't currently own.

Choose how you want to receive your dividends and capital gains:

◉ Reinvest in fund   ○ Deposit in my account

Trading Password: [✶✶✶✶✶✶]

(PREVIEW ORDER) (CLEAR) (CANCEL ORDER)

Step 2a. Select Dollars; or Shares; or Dollars, but no fractional shares.

- If you select Dollars, you'll be investing a specific amount of money from your account in the mutual fund—when the trade settles, you'll own that dollar amount worth of shares in the fund. You could end up buying a portion of a share (fractional shares) because the amount of money you specified didn't equal a whole number of shares.

- If you select Shares, you'll be purchasing a specific number of shares in the fund. Your account will be debited for an amount that equals the number of shares multiplied by the net asset value (NAV) of a single share. If you are buying a fund with a front-end load, the number of shares you specify will be multiplied by the public offer price (POP).

- If you select Dollars, but no fractional shares, E✶TRADE places your order for as many whole shares as the money you specify will purchase. When you review the order, you may find that your account is charged for somewhat less than the dollar amount you specified.

PAYING YOURSELF A DIVIDEND

The automatic reinvestment of dividends and capital gains in mutual funds is one of the great conveniences of the investment world. Without lifting a finger (or even thinking about it) you are maintaining a regular investment program and advancing steadily toward your investment goals.

Step 2b. Enter the amount you want to buy. Make sure you have enough cash in your account to cover the purchase. If you are buying shares in a fund that you don't currently own, you will have to specify how you want your fund income handled. There are two choices:

- **Reinvest in fund.** Your dividends and capital gains (proceeds from asset sales within a fund) will be automatically used to purchase more shares in the same fund for dollar cost averaging and tax purposes, rather than taking them as earned income.

- **Deposit in my account.** Your dividend and capital gains distributions from the mutual fund company will be credited to your account as earned income.

Step 2c. Type your trading password, then click Preview Order.

Step 3. On the Preview page, review the information carefully. If you entered everything correctly, click Place Order. To cancel or change your order, click Cancel Order.

Step 4. The order confirmation page provides a summary of your order and the order number for your records.

Preview Fund Order

Step ❸

Account Number: 8889-2212

Verify that your order is correct and click the Place Order button below:

Time: February 18, 2000 6:13 PM EST

Amount: $2500.00

Fund Name and Symbol: Buy JANUS ENTERPRISE FUND (JAENX)

Reinvestment Choice: Reinvest dividends and capital gains

Commission: This fund participates in E*TRADE's no-transaction fee program. You pay no sales charges or transaction fees for this order. If you sell this fund within 30 days of purchase, a transaction fee will apply upon sale. E*TRADE receives compensation from the fund companies paticipating in the no-load/no-transaction fee program.

Pricing: This order will be priced as of close of the next market day.

Review your order carefully. You are placing a firm order.

PLACE ORDER   **CANCEL ORDER**

Mutual Fund Order Confirmation

Account Number: 8889-2212

Your buy order is accepted.

Thank you for your order to **buy** the JANUS ENTERPRISE FUND (JAENX).

Time: 6:20 PM EST 2/18/00

Order Number: 157

Amount of Order: $2500.00

Pricing: This order will be priced as of close of the next market day.

Exchanging Mutual Fund Shares Online

Sometimes you want to switch your mutual fund shares to another fund in the same fund family. To do this, you must execute what's called an exchange. (If you are switching to a fund in a different fund family, the selling and buying are handled as separate transactions, as outlined previously.)

Step 1. From the Trading area, click Enter Order under the Mutual Funds heading. Select Exchange funds. Select a fund name from among those you own, then click Sell.

Step 2. Enter an amount that you want to sell.

- If you want to sell all your shares in this mutual fund, click All I own.
- If you want to sell a dollar amount, select Dollars and enter an amount. This means that E*TRADE will place an order to redeem as many shares as equals the dollars you enter. When you do this, you may sell parts of shares in addition to whole shares.
- If you want to sell a number of shares, select Shares and enter the number you want to sell.

Step 3. Click Continue and find the fund from the same mutual fund family that you want to buy. Click the Buy link next to the fund. If you are buying shares in a fund that you currently don't hold in your account, specify whether you want to reinvest dividends and capital gains. (See Buying Mutual Fund Shares Online, earlier in this chapter.)

Step 4. Review your exchange order carefully. Enter your trading password, then click Preview Order.

Step 5. Check your order and click Place Order if you wish to finalize the exchange. If you would like to cancel or change your order, you must do it at this point. To change the order, click Cancel Order.

CHAPTER 15

Keeping
Track

W hat are you worth right this minute? To the penny? Do you know that? Unless you have your whole portfolio with an online financial service provider, you can't possibly know for sure.

The power of online investing is the power of control. It shifts your money management activity from a reactive stance to a proactive relationship.

- If you have an online account, you can evaluate and monitor your investments any time you want.

- If you have an online account, you can easily and clearly understand just how your investments are doing compared to the market—and how they would be doing if you had made other choices.

- If you have an online account, you can run projections to see how different financial alternatives would impact your investments.

- If you have an online account, your computer (or your cell phone or pager) can alert you whenever there is a change in your investments—whether or not you're watching them.

> **"** Online investing allows me to invest at times that are convenient for me, without having to wait. **"**
>
> K.D., Online Investor

Are you getting the power and potential of this online investing stuff?

Connected to a network of online financial information and services, you have the power to be smarter and more in control of your money than anyone at any time in the history of the world.

By having your account with an online financial service provider, your investments are connected all the time. The second that E*TRADE gets the latest stock market quotes, we update every account. For every financial investment.

As soon as we get the information, your portfolio reflects that change. Suddenly, you're not looking at a statement of what was, you're looking at a statement of what is!

Think about that and what it can mean to your investment goals and strategy. No, don't think about it—I'll tell you: Whether you've got one account with multiple holdings or multiple accounts with one holding, online account and portfolio management tools give you a complete picture. Any day. Any time of day.

(Once again, the examples here are specific to E*TRADE, but other financial service providers may have similar options.)

Account Balances. Log on to your account. You've got an up-to-the-minute reading of the value of all securities held in your account, your total **account equity**, and your **buying power** for making future investments. You don't have to enter any numbers, and you don't have to do any calculations. It's all there. That's never been possible before!

Account Positions. Check your **account positions**. You've got a summary of the current financial stake in each of your investments held in that particular account. That's never been possible before!

Account Activity. Review every entry that's been made from cash or margin investing, as well as any dividends earned,

account equity
The total amount of assets (cash and fully-owned securities) in an account minus any liabilities (amounts borrowed and still owed).

buying power
In a margin account, the maximum dollar amount of marginable securities the account holder can purchase or sell short without depositing more funds.

account positions
The quantity and market value of each security held in an account.

deposits and reinvestments made, and interest charges to your account right up to the most recent day. That's never been possible before! (Are you starting to get my drift?)

Account Trading History. See every transaction entered, executed, changed or cancelled in your account, including any trades executed today.

Account Tax Records. See the year-to-date tax situation of your account, including capital gains and other fiscal statements you'll need for IRS planning and reporting—to the minute—so you can make any end-of-year adjustments or plan tax-saving strategies for the year.

No More Paper

Once upon a time you had no choice but to receive a paper confirmation in your mailbox every time you bought or sold a stock, bond or mutual fund. Like paper? Have it your way. But for those who prefer an electronic filing system, some financial service providers, like E*TRADE, are now offering all-electronic versions of trade confirmations, statements and cleared checks. It's the future—now.

Online Trade Confirmation

B–You Bought S–You Sold	Description	Price	Amount	Interest or Sales Tax	Sec. Fee and/or Broker Assisted	Commission	Net Amount
B 100	IBM	112.25	11,225.00	0	0	$14.95	11,239.95

Account Number	Acct. Type	Trans. Type	Trade Date	Settlement Date	Symbol	CUSIP	
1234-5678	2	06	01-27-2000	01-31-2000	IBM	459200-01-1	Unsolicited

Portfolio Tracking

Online portfolios can include sets of securities that you own or a group that you're just "watching." An online portfolio is really a powerful tracking tool—a quick scoreboard of how you're doing overall or a quick comparison of how each security in your portfolio is performing. And beyond all that, online portfolio management gives you the power to select what you want to look at—and how you want to view it.

Portfolio Manager

Account Portfolio: 8889-2212   February 18, 2000   1:34 PM ET

Views: Quick View I **Performance** I Research I Option Watch I My View

- Create New List
- Create New View

Symbol		Last Trade		Holdings		Gain/Loss		Market	More
		Price	Chg	Qty	Paid	$	%	Value	Info
GM	Trade	$73\frac{9}{16}$	$-\frac{9}{16}$	50	85.56	$-600	-14.0%	$3,678	News Chart
WMT	Trade	$48\frac{1}{2}$	$+\frac{1}{8}$	75	47	$113	+3.2%	$3,638	News Chart
CSCO	Trade	$129\frac{3}{4}$	$-\frac{3}{4}$	75	$66\frac{1}{4}$	$4,763	+95.9%	$9,731	News Chart
EBAY	Trade	$140\frac{7}{8}$	$-4\frac{3}{8}$	75	$112\frac{15}{16}$	$2,095	+24.7%	$10,566	News Chart
RSEGX	Trade	$77.76	$2.04	200	$36.63	$8,228	+112.3%	$15,554	News Chart
BCLTX	Trade	$10.43	$0.00	500	$11.72	$-640	-10.9%	$5,220	News Chart
				Performance Summary:		$13,959	35.2%	$48,387	

Add Entries I Edit Watch List I Update Prices I Show News   **Real-time quotes**

Select Views. At some online financial service providers, this option gives you the power to choose what information you want to look at for each security listed in your portfolio(s).

Pick the perspective you want. Want it simple? Just look at the basics for each security—current price, dollar/percentage change in price, and volume traded that day. As you get more experienced, you can switch to a performance view that includes a much wider range of data. Or you can customize your view to include just the data you're interested in.

Whichever view you select, your online portfolio links you to all the latest market news and charts on the holdings or prospects you're tracking—a powerful tool for following trends in securities and the markets.

If that was all you could do, even if you couldn't invest online, research online, or invest online, those features alone would make an online account the most powerful fiscal tool you've ever had.

Sound good? Just wait, it gets better. Your online account comes with one of the most truly brilliant features ever invented: The ability to be automatically notified (via email, pager or digital cell phone) when an order you've placed has been executed or when a stock price or index hits a particular target you've set.

Setting Alerts

Imagine having a personal assistant monitoring all your investments 24 hours a day and letting you know the moment an important change happens. And the best thing is—you decide what's important. That's an alert.

Setting Up Alerts. You can set alerts at any time on any account—to monitor the markets and inform you of any changes. You can set the alert to advise you whenever you log onto your online account or you can set it to e-mail you at any address you designate (including your alpha-numeric pager). Whether your strategy is damage control, identifying opportunities, or both, all you have to do is specify the conditions you're interested in for each security you're monitoring.

For example, you might specify an increase or decrease in price to a certain level, an increase or decrease to a certain P/E ratio, or a volume of shares traded in a single

THE ELECTRONIC WATCHDOG

When there's been a change in your investments in the past, who notified whom? When was the last time you got an unsolicited phone call from your bricks and mortar broker or financial advisor telling you she saw a change in the market and checked your portfolio to assess your position? Most likely, never. Usually what happens is you read about a change in the market and, nervously, you call your broker to find out what's happened to your money. Alerts give you the control no individual investor has ever had before. By setting alerts on all your investments, you can be notified immediately of any changes. By the electronic device of your choice. The moment it happens.

Alert Me When

Symbol: YHOO   **Type:** Stock ▾   **Delivery:** Inbox ▾

Price: ☐ rises to $	☐ falls to $	
☐ up by	%	☑ down by	20	%
Vol: ☐ reaches	shares	
P/E: ☐ rises to	☐ falls to	

SUBMIT >   CANCEL

day. Or you can specify conditions to keep an electronic eye watching all three categories—price, P/E, and volume, at once. The alert will monitor each security for the conditions you're looking for and send you an instant message the moment the event occurs so you can take appropriate action.

At E*TRADE, you can also set up alerts to tell you when trades have been executed, if an order has expired or been rejected, or to notify you of a margin call.

But the real power of alerts is fully realized when you combine them with the next feature:

Create Watch Lists

Your portfolio can be a list of the securities you hold or a list of securities you're just thinking about investing in. Think of it as a personal digital financial assistant. You might have one portfolio or ten. It doesn't matter—it can be whatever is best for your needs. You can create as many lists as you want, in any way that works best for you. For example, you can:

DIFFERENT EGGS, DIFFERENT BASKETS

Besides spreading your risk across different securities, you should also consider different portfolios for different needs. The government requires that you keep your IRA, Keogh, and SEP accounts separate from your regular investment accounts. You should also consider separate portfolios for your children, your spouse, and for special purposes such as college funds or sabbaticals. Your kids' portfolios can tolerate higher risk than yours can. So, why not invest accordingly? Sometimes, by separating your funds into different portfolios, you discover that you can tolerate different levels of risk in each.

- Create an IRA portfolio for tracking all your investments in your IRA account.
- Create a portfolio for tracking different positions in one stock or all your holdings in a specific industry sector.
- Monitor securities you don't own but that you might like to own some day.
- Compare performance trends of a single security or a number of securities against each other, or against the market as a whole.

The more you focus or trim your lists, the more watch lists can help you meet your financial goals.

> **WHOM DO YOU TRUST?**
> Watch lists are the perfect way to filter information. As you scour the Internet for investment ideas, you can create a tracking portfolio of A-list hot prospects—then see how they do over time.

Watch List

February 24, 2000   1:05 PM ET

Watch Lists: Favorite Portfolio I **My Watch List** I Sample Watch List
Views: Quick View I **Performance** I Research I Option Watch

- Create New List
- Create New View

Symbol		Last Trade	Change $	%	Volume	More Info
LU	Trade	$58^3{}_4$	$+1^7{}_8$	+3.55%	15412500	News Chart Profile Financials Analysts Options
AOL	Trade	$59^3{}_4$	$+1^7{}_{16}$	+2.47%	33025400	News Chart Profile Financials Analysts Options
TOM	Trade	$11^{11}{}_{16}$	$-{}^5{}_{16}$	−2.60%	561300	News Chart Profile Financials Analysts Options
DAL	Trade	$47^1{}_8$	$+{}^5{}_8$	+1.34%	424000	News Chart Profile Financials Analysts Options
PFE	Trade	$32^{11}{}_{16}$	$-1^5{}_{16}$	−3.86%	4922400	News Chart Profile Financials Analysts Options
ORCL	Trade	$61^1{}_4$	$-1^{13}{}_{16}$	−2.87%	20641800	News Chart Profile Financials Analysts Options
AMZN	Trade	$67^5{}_8$	$-2^{13}{}_{16}$	−3.99%	3779400	News Chart Profile Financials Analysts Options
YHOO	Trade	$165^3{}_{16}$	$-1^1{}_{64}$	−0.61%	5082800	News Chart Profile Financials Analysts Options
MSFT	Trade	$93^7{}_8$	$-{}^3{}_8$	−0.40%	19916800	News Chart Profile Financials Analysts Options

Add Entries I Edit Watch List I Update Prices I Show News   **Real-time quotes**

Watch lists /tracking portfolios give you the power to assess your risk comfort level.

What level of risk can you really tolerate? A tracking portfolio can help you figure that out. Got a security you think isn't so secure? Put it in a tracking portfolio and watch what it does. More importantly, *notice how you feel about what it does.* Do you mind the ups and downs of the tracking portfolio? Are the levels of risk acceptable—or do you monitor them more closely than you want? Do you find yourself saying "If only I'd actually bought (or sold) that stock"?

The wonder of the investment markets is that there is no such thing as "woulda, coulda, shoulda." There are only opportunities. And if you missed one, another one will come along. *It always does.* How you feel about your tracking portfolio(s) can go a long way to helping you identify those opportunities.

> **"** The major advantage to online investing is being able to control my own funds—which have performed better than my managed accounts at full-commission brokers. **"**
>
> E.P., Physician

Are You Ready to Be Part of the Revolution?

Bodacious. (I had to get that word in here somewhere— even though Cheri Oteri of *Saturday Night Live* keeps telling me to "give it a rest.") We've both done our jobs and now it's up to you. Now you've got a taste of the ease, the power, and the potential of going online and taking control of your financial life. But don't get too cocky. There's a lot more to learn—but you've got to start somewhere.

Start with as little as you like. No one said this was an all-or-nothing deal. Open an online account with a portion of your assets and keep any old twentieth-century accounts you already have. As you get more comfortable online, become more confident in your own decision-making, and rely less on other people to manage your money, you can transfer out of the accounts that are costing you too much or aren't serving your investment needs.

As I said in my opening paragraph, over the last four years, more than 15 million people made a choice—to be part of an extraordinary future that's unfolding around us. I believe in the revolution and the empowerment it's going to bring to every human being on this planet. I invite you to come along—it's going to be a fantastic ride! Never forget—with empowerment comes responsibility and accountability. After all, *it's your money.*

Step V:
High
Gear

Have I told you all there is to know about investing and managing your money online? Not even close! But as I said, you've got enough to get started. As you get more comfortable, there are a few more sophisticated research and investment techniques you should know about. I'll cover them in brief, but I urge you to carefully consider my "rules" for this section:

1. If you don't understand this section, don't try anything in it. You'll just get burned.

2. If you don't understand this section, don't let it stop you from investing online. Many people have invested successfully without using these techniques.

3. If anything in this section interests you, *learn more about it.* What I've written here is a simple overview, not a complete how to. The deeper you go, the more knowledge you need to have in order to succeed.

CHAPTER 16

Your
Options

You've heard about options. You may have heard friends talk about making large profits from small investments. You're interested in trading options. Uh-huh.

I'll make you a deal. You can read this introduction to options. You can research options on our Web site. But you have to make me a promise: *You will not invest in options until you've gone to the Chicago Board Options Exchange Web site* (www.cboe.com), *and downloaded and read "The Characteristics and Risks of Standardized Options".*

You should also read at least two other books on the subject. There are plenty of good books about options. I've listed a couple in the bibliography. But that's the point: Options are very risky and very esoteric. There are whole books written on the subject. Lots of books. I can give you an overview and a basic understanding of options in this chapter, but you won't learn enough here to safely invest in them. Got it?

> **TAKE A TRIP TO CHICAGO**
> Stock options first started trading in 1973 at the Chicago Board Options Exchange—and they've got one of the best Web sites for options. If you're looking for the online resource for information and materials for options, their Web site at *www.cboe.com* is a gold mine of rules, risks, and details. Check them out.

Okay, here goes:

To understand options, you've got to put aside just about all the information I've already given you. Why? Because options are different from stocks and bonds in a number of important ways.

1. Options speak their own language. Although the word options means what it says, you have options or choices you can exercise—the language of options is unique to these markets and needs to be mastered. **Calls**. **Puts**. Spreads. Straddles. These are just a few of the terms (and strategies) that are used in option trading.

2. Options are not securities. A stock is a share of a company, "secured" by the value of the company. **An option is the right to buy (or sell) a stock (or some other security) on or before a given time for a specified price.** Read that again very carefully. It's not the stock itself, it's the right to buy or sell the stock on or before a given time for a given price. (I'll explain how this works in more detail later.) Its value is derived from the underlying stock. That's why options are also called *derivatives*.

3. Options have time limits. Besides the right to buy or sell a stock, an option has a time component. You have the right to buy or sell a stock up to a given date. After that date, the option is worthless. That's right, I said worthless.

4. Options can produce an attractive rate of return in a short time on a small investment — but you can also lose every penny you put in. You can get better leverage with a smaller investment than you can trading stock. But there are certain types of options trading where you can lose more, much more than you put in—although certain financial service providers like E*TRADE don't allow this.

5. Options trading is not a "trial and error" form of investing. You shouldn't consider investing in options until you've had significant experience investing in stocks. Financial service providers have strict rules and eligibility

call
The right to buy a specified amount of the underlying security at a specified price on or before an expiration date.

put
An options contract with the right to sell a specified amount of the underlying security at a specified price on or before an expiration date.

requirements for trading options because of the risks involved.

6. Options have only been traded since the early 1970s.

Unlike stocks and bonds, which have been traded back and forth for hundreds of years, standardized options have only been around since the 1970s. A lot of people still view options trading as an Alice in Wonderland phenomenon that they just don't understand. That's okay, and it's why I wrote this chapter—but you might get confused, and your friends in the office might get just as confused when you try to explain it to them. Take it easy, take it slow, and make sure you understand this stuff before you try to trade. It's easier to learn this now, the easy way, than the hard way when things go wrong.

7. Basic principles don't change. Stocks, bonds, options:

No matter what we're talking about, we're still talking about the three basic rules of investing: 1) Someone wants to put your money to work for you; 2) Return is measured in two ways: return on investment and rate of return; and 3) The greater the risk, the greater the potential reward. With options, the person who wants to put your money to work for you is yourself.

Finally, there's your own personality to consider. Trading options requires that you pay attention. Options have a time limit. You can't just purchase an option, put it in your portfolio, and look at it a week before it's supposed to expire. You've got to constantly monitor its **intrinsic value** and **time value**. (I'll explain those, too.) Options trading takes courage, attention, and the ability to take a punch. You have to know when it's best to cut your losses. In fact, Kenny Rogers pretty much summed it up: "You gotta know when to hold 'em, know when to fold 'em." If you're not the type of person who can constantly tend your eggs—if you're the type of person who wants to "set it and forget it," then options trading isn't for you.

Have I scared you off? Good. If I have, and you already

know your risk tolerance level and personality aren't up for this, skip this chapter and keep going. Not scared yet? Then read on.

Let me repeat: An option is not a security. If you buy an **option contract**, you buy *the right to take some action.* In some cases, options can also obligate you to perform some action. Ever put $100 down on a car or a piece of furniture with the understanding that if you bought it, the $100 would be applied to the price, but if you walked away from the deal, the seller could keep the $100 and you wouldn't be responsible for actually buying the car or the furniture? That $100 contract is an option.

Stay with this analogy. One day you're reading an auto enthusiast's magazine, and you read about a new sports car coming out next year. You love what you see. You think: *This car is going to be in such demand, people will pay money above the sticker price to own one.* So, you go to the dealer and you make him an offer:

"Y'know that new car you'll be selling next year? The suggested retail price is going to be $25,000. I'll give you $100 now if you give me the right to buy the car at that price 12 months from now. If I decide not to buy the car, you keep the $100."

What's the dealer think? "Hmmm, what can I really lose with this deal? If the car's popularity meets expectations and it sells for $25,000, this guy will either buy the car at that price or walk away from the deal. I either make $25,000 or $100 for doing nothing. On the other hand, if the car is so unpopular that I have to reduce the price to $23,000 for people to buy it, he's stuck: He either pays me the full $25,000 per our contract or he walks away from the deal and, again, I keep the $100. If the car's so hot that people bid the price up to $27,000 just to get one, well, I lose $1,900 (the extra $2,000 I could have gotten minus the

option contract
For stock options, one option contract equals an option to buy or sell 100 shares of the under-lying stock (for a specified price on or before and expi-ration date).

WHEN TIME RUNS OUT
Unlike stocks, options don't last indefi-nitely. On the third Saturday of every month, all the options for that month are expired, exercised or assigned. Options that expire are declared void. Options that are exercised or assigned are traded as part and parcel of the contract. This happens automatically if the stock is trad-ing at least 3/4 of a point better than the strike price (see sidebar on facing page).

extra $100 I'm getting for the option) by making this deal. On the other hand, I've got a guaranteed sale of at least $25,000." So the dealer looks at you and says "Sure."

This exchange illustrates the "hedging" quality of options. By the way you buy and sell options and the way the dealer buys and sells options, each can manage his or her potential gains and losses in the market. (We'll go over this in more detail, but for now, let's stay with the basics.)

You walk out of the dealer's showroom with a contract in your pocket. That contract is the option (purchased for $100) to buy the car or walk away from the deal 12 months from now. It's not the car. You've just bought an option and the dealer just sold an option. The dealer's speculating, too. He's hoping the actual selling price of the car will be equal or less than what you agreed to pay him in the option contract, and that he'll be able to pocket what you paid for the option.

> **YOUR OPTIONS ASSIGNMENT**
>
> If you hold an option that's at least 3/4 of a point in the money (could be traded for a profit) at expiration, it's going to be exercised or assigned. What's that mean? Let's go back to the car analogy. Let's say the car is worth more than the option price. If you still held the option at the expiration date, the dealer would in effect sell the car to you—and you'd pay the purchase (strike) price. Your option would be *exercised* and the dealer (the seller of the option) would be *assigned*.

Four months pass and word of this car starts to appear in the general press. You hear people talking about how hot this car will be. Now you start thinking about the option in your pocket. "Hmmm. If someone thinks he or she will have to pay $27,000 for that car, then this contract is worth a lot more than $100. With this contract, someone would only have to pay $25,000 for the car instead of $27,000. So the value of this option contract is $2,000."

Suddenly, the option contract has a value all its own. It's different from the value of the car it can buy, but it still has some value. As the option's expiration date approaches, however, that value may change based on changes in the car's expected selling price.

That's what we mean when we say an option has an **intrinsic value** and a **time value**. Although you can exercise the option anytime up to the expiration date, the closer you get to that date, the more time becomes a factor in calculating the price.

If the "premium" over the $25,000 sticker price keeps rising, the value of your option will keep rising. If it looks like the car will sell for $25,000 or less, your option will likely become worthless.

Lesson One About Options

You don't actually have to buy the stock (the car in this example) to make money. You can "trade" the value of the option without ever having owned the actual security.

Back to the analogy. Anytime up to the option's expiration date, you have several choices: You can sell the option for a profit or loss, walk away from the whole deal (let the option expire), or exercise the option and take delivery of the car. Each has its particular advantages and disadvantages.

1. Sell the option for a profit. If everyone believes that the car will sell for more than the sticker price, they'll bid the value of the option up. At any point you could take the money and run.

2. Sell the option for a loss. As the date of expiration approaches, it looks like the car might sell for slightly more or less than $25,000. Suddenly your $100 doesn't look like such a great deal. But there might be someone who's thinking *If I pay this guy $50 for his $100 option, what do I lose? The car only has to sell for $25,051 for this to be a good deal on my part.* If you think the car will sell for its sticker price or below, you might want to cut your losses and get out for $50.

3. Let the option expire. You're not sure up to the last day which way the car will go. On the date the contract expires, the dealer calls you up and says, "Want the car?" You're thinking to yourself, *Well, it's not as nice a deal as I thought it would be a year ago*, so you say no, the option time limit expires, and you lose the entire $100. This is still better than being stuck with a $25,000 car you might never like.

4. Exercise the option. In other words, buy the car. The car is in demand. People are offering the dealer $27,000 for the car. You decide to exercise your option, buy the car for $25,000, and resell it to someone else for $27,000. Now your profit on the option is $1,900 (your $25,000 purchase price deducted from the $27,000 sale price is $2,000, but you paid $100 for that opportunity, so your net profit is $1,900).

Now Do You See Why People Want to Trade Options?

The car example is similar to buying a *call option*. The call is the right to buy a stock for a specific price up until a specific date in the future. Buying a call simply means you're buying the right to buy the stock.

As the date of the call expiration approaches, you've got to make a decision: basically the same four choices you had with the car. You can sell the option for a profit or loss, let the option expire, or exercise the option.

That's buying a call. What's selling a call? A call is the right to buy a stock for a specific price until a specific time. Selling a call means you're selling that right (option) to buy the stock. A different analogy may make it easier to explain:

You own a house. You've lived in it a few years and you know that next year you're going to be moving. You paid $120,000 for the house and it's currently worth $150,000. If you could sell the house today, you know you'd make a $30,000 profit, but what's going to happen in a year? Will real estate prices be up? Down? You know you've got to sell the house then, so you won't have the luxury of "waiting out" a down market.

You sell someone an option to buy your house from you in a year for $150,000. That's selling a call—and it's got two powerful benefits for the seller:

1. Increase Your Profits. A year from now, the house is still worth $150,000—but someone paid you $5,000 for the

> **❝** I trade options; having real-time quotes and pre-market hours trading information helps me a great deal and makes my investments easier to follow. **❞**
>
> A.C., Business Manager

option. You make the $5,000 plus the $30,000 profit. You turn over the house (which you needed to do anyway) with the profit from the sale and the profit from the option.

2. Hedge Your Investment. Even if the value of the house jumps to $175,000 that year, you have to sell it for $150,000. In this scenario, you've missed out on an unexpected $25,000 in the selling price of the house. But you still made $30,000 on the house plus $5,000 for the option and you had that profit "locked in" as soon as you sold the option. That's the "hedge" component of options. By carefully analyzing the value of your stocks and the value of different options, you can protect your profits.

The Basics of Calls

Now you understand how it works with analogies, but how does it work on the stock market? Exactly the same way—with some extra terminology thrown in.

1. The general rule is that every call is the right to buy exactly 100 shares.

2. Every call has a strike price. That's the fixed price at which the call allows you to buy the stock for any given security, there may be any number of calls with different expiration dates and different strike prices (an **options chain**), but the expiration date and strike price for any one particular call never changes (except with a stock split).

options chain
A list of options contracts, puts and calls, available in the current time period.

3. Every strike price is set at a regular interval. Rather than trying to offer options at every conceivable price, many options are offered in increments of $5—as in $5, $10, $100, $105, etc. Some will be in increments of $2.50; others (such as index options) can represent $10s or $100s.

4. The dollar sign is dropped when talking about calls, and the strike price is referred to without the dollars. A call with a strike price "at 60" is the option to buy 100 shares of that stock for $60 a share any time up to the expiration date of the option.

5. Every option has a fixed time limit. Stock options stop trading the Friday before the third Saturday of the month; index options expiring that month stop trading the Thursday before the third Saturday.

If you buy a call, it's because you believe that the price of the stock will go up in the future. Just like the car analogy, you would have the same strategy with a call option. Say you bought a call six months ago. You paid $300 for an option with a strike price at 60. That means you have paid $300 for the right to buy 100 shares of the stock for $60 a share. It's now two months from the expiration of the option and the stock is trading for $67 a share. The option is selling for $800. You can sell the call for $800—realizing a net profit of $500. Or you can exercise the call and buy the stock for $60 a share—realizing a profit of $400 ($700 profit on the stock minus the $300 you paid for the option). By exercising, you miss out on $100. In both cases, you profited because the price of the underlying stock did, in fact, go up. If the price had gone down, you would have taken a loss (up to the full cost of the option).

Writing (selling) a call works in reverse. You're selling the right for someone else to buy a stock at a future date. You will be obligated to sell the stock at the strike price if the buyer of your call chooses to exercise the option. You might sell a call if you believe the value of the stock will drop in the future.

1. When you own the stock, writing a call becomes a way to make some extra profits. Let's say you paid $51 a share for the stock. It's now at $60. You sell a call at 60 for six months out for $300. If the stock drops to $58, you've still got an **unrealized gain** (paper profits) of $700 ($5800 minus the $5100 you paid for the stock) plus a **realized gain** (actual profits) of $300 for the call for a combined gain of $1000.

2. When you own the stock, selling a call becomes a way to hedge your losses. Let's say you paid $55 a share for the stock. It's now at $60. You sell a call at 60 for six months out for $300. When the call expires, the stock is selling for $54, so you make $200 instead of losing $100! (You lost $100 on the value of the stock, but you sold the call six months earlier for $300 for a net gain of $200.)

3. What if I didn't own the stock? This would be considered a naked position, or an uncovered call. We don't allow this at E*TRADE, nor do many other online financial service providers, because it's incredibly risky. If the stock moved upward against you, the potential loss to you is unlimited— maybe even beyond your ability to cover it.

Are you thinking "why doesn't everyone trade in options instead of stocks?" Because there are situations where you don't do as well with options. Take the preceding example. Let's say you own a stock that you paid $51 for and you sell a call for $300 at 60 at six months out. But what if the stock is actually selling for $75 when the call is exercised? You have to deliver the stock you paid $51 for to cover the call. Sure, you made $1200 ($900 on the stock and $300 for the call), but you lost the opportunity to make an additional $1500 if you just owned the stock!

When you buy a call, your total risk is the cost of the option, but when you sell a covered call, your total risk is having to sell the stock. But what if you believe the price of the stock will go down—and you don't have any shares, or don't want to sell yours?

Buying a Put

If you understand the basics of calls, you'll see that puts are just the opposite. But a lot of folks get the basic concept of a call, and then get to puts and find themselves lost in the woods looking for grandmother's house.

Puts are the option to sell an underlying stock up until a date and time in the future at a contracted price. You *buy a put* if you believe the value of a stock will go down in the future, and you might *sell a put* if you believe the value of the stock will go up and you want to hedge your potential gains or losses. Your downside risk is exactly reversed from the position you had with a call. As the buyer of a put, your risk exposure is the cost of the option. As the seller of a put, your risk is the difference between the strike price and zero. In addition, if you sell a put and you are assigned, you will need to own or buy the stock in order to cover your position.

Which Way Is up?

Did I lose you?

If you think a stock is going to go up in the future, you could either buy a call or sell a put. In general, you'd buy a call to profit from the stock movement without actually having to buy the stock. If the stock goes down, by buying a call you can lose up to the value of the option. If you sold a put, you can lose whatever it takes to cover the put, including being forced to buy your stock at an unfavorable price.

If you think a stock is going to go down in the future, you could either buy a put or sell a covered call. In general, you'd buy a put to profit from the stock movement without actually having to *short* the stock, and you'd sell a call to lock in your profits or minimize your losses if you already owned the underlying stock. If the stock goes up, by buying a put you can lose up to the value of the option. If you sold a call, you could be forced to sell your stock at an inferior price.

Beyond Puts and Calls

There are still two more options that I haven't told you about yet; you're probably going to hear about them from somebody else, though, and think I was holding out on you. So, I'm going to talk to you a little about both. If you get lost, just move on to what's next and forget this section completely.

One strategy is called a *straddle*. A straddle is something you use when you think the stock is going to move big, but you don't know in what direction. Let's say you hear about a new car but you don't know if it's the next Porsche or the next DeLorean. You buy a call and a put with the same strike price. If the value of the car moves way up, your call is worth money, and your put isn't; if the car's a lemon, your put is worth more, and your call isn't. So long as the price fluctuates enough to cover the cost of both premiums, you make money. This example illustrates a *long straddle*.

How does this work with a stock? Let's say you hear that TriMount Studios is about to come out with a new blockbuster movie called *Blow'd Up*. It could be the next *Star Wars*; it could be the next *Waterworld*. You don't know. You're hoping it'll be one or the other, so you decide to enter in a long straddle. You buy both a put and a call on the stock. If the lines for the movie are around the block, profits go up, the stock rises, your call's in the money—and so are you. If cobwebs are growing on the seats, the stock falls—and your put's a winner.

Still confused? Let's put it into numbers. Suppose that TriMount is trading right now at 50. You buy a 50 put option for 2, and a 50 call option for 3. You've paid a total of 5 so far.

If the stock moves less than 5 points either way, you will not make money. Whatever you do make won't offset what you paid for the options.

If the stock moves more than 5 points either way, you'll make money—no matter if the stock moves up (in which case your call is worth money, but your put is not) or if the stock moves down (in which case your put is worth money, and your call is not).

Finally, there are spreads; I really don't even want to go into these in this book. If you're still with me after this one, I'm going to be really impressed. As I said, though, you might as well hear it here first.

A *spread* is when you buy an option (obtain a right) and simultaneously sell another option (take on an obligation)

ANALYZE THIS AND TRACK THAT

One of the powers of online investing is the ability to track securities you haven't actually bought. In Chapter 15 you'll find a detailed explanation of setting up and running a tracking portfolio.

with the same underlying security. Spreads are extremely complex. And you have to be very, very experienced to understand how they work and how to trade them successfully. At least now you have some idea of what they are.

Intense, isn't it? That's why there's so much more scrutiny and stricter requirements if you want to trade options.

Do you think you understand options? Fine. Now remember your promise to me. Go learn some more, and when you feel comfortable, give them a try in your tracking portfolio before trading them for real.

Researching Option Risk and Reward Online

You research stock options online in much the same way you do stocks. At E*TRADE, you can enter the symbol for the stock you're interested in. Next to the symbol entry box you can select what to view from a pull-down menu. Click the down arrow and select Options. When you click Go, a set of quotes for all the options contracts available in the current time period (the *options chain*) will appear on your screen.

In choosing to trade options, you should be even more familiar with the company and the market than when investing in stocks. Remember, if you buy a stock and the market moves against you, you still own a percentage of the company. If you buy an option and the market moves against you, you have to make a decision against a specific time limit. So, review company profiles, financial reports, and data charts for the underlying stock very carefully before trading options. Even a good pick can be a loser if the stock does not move enough in your direction by the expiration date.

With dozens of different options (get it?) for every stock, how can you calculate your potential gains and losses over time?

Option Quote

AMZN Apr $70 Call (YQNDN)				February 24, 2000 1:08 PM EST Real-time quote, CBOE
Price $7^3{}_8$	**Change** -2		**Last Trade**	February 24, 2000 1:04 PM EST
Bid $7^3{}_4$	**Ask**	8	**Open Interest**	2190
Premium $7^3{}_8$	**Volume**	62	**Day range**	$7^1{}_4$–$10^1{}_2$
Prev. Close $9^3{}_8$	**Open**	$10^1{}_8$	**Days to Go**	58
Shares Per Contract 100		**52 week range**	$45^1{}_2$ (12/9/1999)—$5^3{}_4$ (2/22/2000)	

Underlying Symbol **AMAZON.COM INC (AMZN)**			Real-time quote, NASDAQ NM
Price	$67^3{}_4$	**Change**	$-2^{11}{}_{16}$ (–3.82%)
Bid	$67^{11}{}_{16}$+	**Ask**	$67^3{}_4$
Bid Size	100	**Ask Size**	900
Volume	3,790,800	**Tick**	n/a
Day range	$65^5{}_8$—$71^3{}_8$	**Open**	$70^9{}_{16}$
52wk Hi	113 (12/9/1999)	**52wk Lo**	41 (8/10/1999)

Black-Scholes analysis

Myron Scholes and Fisher Black were among the first to develop mathematical models that accurately predicted the value of stock options. Most options analysts now use their models, or modified versions, when assessing options values.

Among online financial service providers offering options trading, some also provide options analysis tools. At E*TRADE, we offer options price and leverage analysis as well as **Black-Scholes analysis**. Stop by and do your own price analysis of calls and puts. Just enter the date when you believe the stock will be at the price you're interested in and the dollar amount you want to invest. (You can also enter a volatility percentage and a Treasury bond interest rate in the Advanced section.) This options analysis tool enables you to take into account the underlying stock's price and volatility, the option's strike price and expiration date, interest rates, and dividends in making your risk/reward assessment.

Finally, because option trading is considered highly speculative and not for the inexperienced investor, many online financial service providers, including E*TRADE, require additional account application approval for options trading privileges before investors can place an options order.

"Okay, Christos, what do I do with all this information on options?"

Nothing. Keep it all in mind. As you get more skilled at investing and learn more about options, you might be able to use them to help reach your target number. How? Here's one simple example:

Let's say ten years ago you bought 10,000 shares of a stock at $10. Today, it's worth $45—a $350,000 paper profit. But the stock hasn't moved up or down much in over a year. That portion of your portfolio isn't working to help you "make your number." You're not concerned about the stock falling wildly, but you'd like to make some extra money while you take your profits and move that money into something else that can work harder. Every few months, you sell a call for 1,000 shares. If the stock goes up, you don't complain. You deliver those 1,000 shares; you still make your $35 a share profit, still make money on the call, and still have 9,000 shares that have increased in value. If the stock stays flat or drops, you gain profit from the premium of the call, making a "flat" investment work for you.

> **I'VE GOT YOU COVERED**
> A covered call is an options contract whose writer owns the shares of stock contracted for at the strike price and has them available to sell. This was the "hedging" function of options we talked about.

CHAPTER 17

Stock Investing 2.0

I n Chapter 12, we talked about the basics of stock analysis —the fundamental numbers you should identify and track, the information you can gather and review. Remember, you've got two objectives when you research: finding an investment that looks like it meets your objectives and doing as much research as you can to determine whether its future results will match or exceed its past performance. Knowledge is power. There's a lot more you can learn about stocks—and a lot more information that's now available online to individual investors like you. As you become more comfortable with the data and the process of researching stocks online, there are many more numbers and strategies you can use to help you make the right choice. I've outlined a few of them in this chapter.

HOLD THE CALCULATOR
You don't have to do all the math yourself. Many of the numbers/ratios discussed in this section can be found online. E*TRADE, like many others, offers detailed company profiles. Just bring up a stock quote, then click on Profile.

Price-to-Cash Flow Ratio

What Is the Price-to-Cash Flow Ratio?
The price-to-cash flow ratio compares the current market value of a company to the company's net cash flow which

equals the company's year-end net income plus depreciation and amortization minus required investment.

How Is This Ratio Used?

This percentage is used by investors as an alternative to a company's price-to-earnings ratio. Whereas earnings are reduced by charges such as depreciation and amortization, cash flows represent a company's cash receipts minus cash payments over a period of time. Price to cash flow is used as a barometer of the stock's value rather than earnings per share relative to changes in the company's cash flow over the past year or more.

Price-to-Sales Ratio

What Is the Price-to-Sales Ratio?

Investors use this value as a yardstick to evaluate the per share value of a stock relative to the company's volume of sales or revenues.

Why Is the Price-to-Sales Ratio Important?

The price-to-sales ratio can often be a better way to compare apples with apples. If you're trying to evaluate which of two companies is stronger in a particular industry, their P/E ratios or EPS might not tell the whole story. One company might have new plants to depreciate or one-time write-offs that can change the EPS or may be investing in marketing to grab a larger piece of market share. By comparing sales figures and then comparing those figures to price, you have a clearer comparison between companies without their differing accounting practices getting in the way. In addition, price-to-sales provides a way to value companies with lots of potential, but have yet to realize earnings. For some Internet companies where heavy investments are being made at the expense of earnings, price-to-sales has proven a useful alternative to price-to-earnings.

> **IT'S ALL IN THE PAST**
>
> The most frequently quoted phrase in investing is "Past performance is no indication of future results." My lawyers made us use it at the beginning of the book, remember? It's a valid statement. Remember the classic statistical problem: If a two-sided coin comes up heads 99 times, what are the odds it will come up heads on the one hundredth toss? The answer is always 50/50. Keep that in mind whenever you look to past performance as a measurement of future possibilities.

Price-to-Book Value Ratio

What Is the Price-to-Book Value Ratio?
This figure compares the current market value of a company to the company's value according to its balance sheet (assets minus liabilities).

You can calculate a company's Price-to-Book Value Ratio yourself by dividing the company's market capitalization by its book value.

What Does the Price-to-Book Value Ratio Tell Me?
The price-to-book value ratio essentially tells you how much more investors value the company as an ongoing entity than as a derived accounting value on paper.

If the stock is selling at a market price below its book value, this may indicate the stock is a good buy. But take note: While market value reflects the current outlook in the marketplace for the stock/company as a reflection of future expectations, book value is primarily an accounting value, based on a set of arbitrary accounting rules that spread certain expenses over a number of years.

Return on Equity (ROE)

What Is Return on Equity?
This one's often seen as a measurement of the true growth rate of a company. It's the stock's year-end EPS divided by its book value. Fundamentally, ROE describes how much equity a company is able to generate using its given base of assets. Logically, a company that is able to generate a lot of income on a minimal amount of capital is doing quite well.

How is this number used?
When comparing companies, a higher ROE usually indicates a healthier, faster-growing company. Historically, an ROE of 15-20 percent indicates the company is growing in a healthy manner; an ROE higher than 20 percent indicates exceptionally strong growth.

Dividend Yield

What Is Dividend Yield?

For stocks that pay dividends, dividend yield is calculated by dividing the dividend payments of the stock at the end of the year by its market price at the beginning of that year. Also called the percent ratio, this figure is the percentage of the stock's price paid as a dividend.

So, What Does This Mean?

For example, if a company paid $1 per share in dividends and the stock price was $100, the dividend yield was 1 percent. As a measure of a stock's current (versus potential) value, many analysts believe dividend yield goes only so far, because emerging companies tend to pour earnings back into the business rather than paying them out to stockholders.

Beta

What Is Beta?

Beta measures the price volatility and risk of an individual stock compared with the price volatility of the market as a whole.

How Is Beta Calculated and What Does It Mean?

Let's say the price of a stock moved up 10 percent and then down 5 percent in a 30-day period. If the rest of the market stayed unchanged, this would be considered a volatile stock. If the entire market (the Nasdaq for example), however, had that same swing in the same period, the stock would look "normal" by comparison. A stock with a beta of 1.0 indicates that the stock's price is on an even keel with the direction the market is moving. A higher or lower beta indicates greater or lesser price volatility and, therefore, risk than the market as a whole is showing.

Researching Technology Stocks Online

The unknowns associated with picking emerging technology stocks are similar to those encountered when buying a new car. Before you even set foot in a dealership, you've probably done your homework. You've picked the type of car you're most interested in, be it convertible, station wagon, or SUV. You've reviewed a number of cars in the same category and have a sense of the most popular models, the sleekest models, the most reliable models, and the best sellers. You've picked the car that you believe is perfect for you, and once you step into the dealership, you're pretty comfortable with your decision. You only begin to second-guess your selection when the engine light starts flashing and the steering wheel freezes up. Despite customer raves and a stellar service record—which you thoroughly researched—you just purchased the lemon of the lot.

Although purchasing a technology stock is decidedly less dramatic, it can involve similar unknowns. Will the company's technology succeed in the marketplace? Will the company go bankrupt while building the next big thing? Will it be able to survive in a crowded product space?

In the eyes of many of today's investors, an alternative set of strategies has emerged for isolating investment opportunities amid a panorama of upstart technology companies. Due to the unknowns associated with many of these companies, a large number of investors feel that a focus beyond more traditional metrics is warranted.

For the most part, these strategies are not remarkably profound and are destined to include a bit of qualitative analysis. In sum, however, technology specific strategies allow for more informed technology investing. In this section, we'll discuss some of the latest and greatest ways to put a "tech slant" on your research.

The Importance of Growth

According to industry experts, the valuation of emerging technology companies is really a matter of sizing up a given company's growth potential. The conventional valuation of technology companies, especially Internet companies, can prove extremely difficult, given that many technology companies have little history, let alone revenue and earnings. Although buying a technology stock based on here-and-now financial data might seem completely bogus, factoring in a company's bright prospects for growth may reveal an undervalued major player. When selecting an investment candidate, you should ask yourself some questions:

What is the market opportunity that the company is targeting?

- How will the size of this opportunity grow over time?
- How does the opportunity correspond to the growth of the sector, or perhaps the total growth of the Internet?

For consumer Web-based Internet companies in particular, subscriber growth has become an important metric. Due to the fact that largely either advertising or commerce often drives Web site revenues, the number of users accessing a given site can lead directly to the company's bottom or top line.

Ones to Watch
Thinking about investing in high tech? There are many useful indexes that track this sector, including the Goldman Sachs Technology Index, the Morgan Stanley High Tech Index, and the Bloomberg U.S. Internet Index.

Cost Is Key

Perhaps one of the most revolutionary implications of the Internet is the medium's ability to radically alter tried and true cost structures. This is markedly visible in the brokerage business, where the all-electronic infrastructure of online brokerages has virtually eliminated the barrier to low-cost, democratized investing. In addition, the Internet enables scalability. Although a brick-and-mortar business may need to build more physical locations or manufacturing plants as demand increases, an Internet company may need only to add to their technology base, while still reaping the benefit of rapidly increasing sales. As the Internet continues to evolve, technology companies that are able to bring revolutionary, cost-efficient products or services to the playing field should warrant the attention of investors.

The Consumer Is The New Royalty

The Internet revolution is redefining the consumption of goods and services. As consumers' purchasing power is increasingly redirected to the all-electronic convenience of the Internet, Web companies are learning the importance of catering to the demands of the consumer. As Internet companies become more and more dependent upon visible revenue for survival, only those companies that provide innovative solutions that attract, empower, and retain large numbers of consumers will prove successful in the long run.

THE COMPETITION IS JUST A CLICK AWAY

The power and convenience of the Internet is putting more and more power in the hands of consumers. Just had a bad experience on a particular Web site? In a couple mouse clicks, you can be doing business with someone else. Just like that. Through email, message boards, opinion polls and all sorts of other Web-based communication tools, an unhappy customer can share his or her experience with millions of people.

Nonstop Innovation

As new access channels and increased bandwidth become hallmarks of the wired world, companies at the top of their game today will be forced to innovate to meet the growing demands of tomorrow. When investing in technology stocks, both a company's ability to innovate and a company's speed of execution must be thoroughly evaluated. A company that falls behind the curve with regard to new technologies, services, and access channels will be unable to compete in a marketplace defined by rapid, nonstop innovation. Companies that are ahead of the curve today may hold the enviable position of defining and owning the most lucrative market opportunities.

It's Crowded Out There

The high technology/ecommerce industry can currently be characterized as a jungle, with tremendous natural resources and potential, but filled with skilled predators and inhabited by more than a few "elephants." Bill Burnham, a pioneer in evaluating the e-commerce industry, offers some insights in his book, *How to Invest in E-Commerce Stocks*:

> "Microsoft's market capitalization alone is almost four times that of the entire ecommerce industry. Other major players, such as IBM and Oracle, are no slouches either. These companies are like elephants: they go where they like, do what they please, and anything in their way gets flattened. Investors in the Ecommerce industry should keep careful track of the elephants and avoid any companies that appear to be in their immediate paths."

Real Revenues

Most people have a pretty good sense that buying into technology stocks is probably riskier than, say, buying a Treasury bond. Few people, however, know how to minimize their risk while still investing in technology. Once you've decided to take the plunge, how do you differentiate among stocks which when viewed together appear to be flying way too high? One word can help: revenue. As we've discussed earlier, historically companies have been valued on how successful they are today, and how successful they will likely become in the future. The easiest way of gauging success in the marketplace is to determine how much money a company is able to generate. In the case of technology companies, it's easy to lose track of which companies are solid, revenue-generating companies today, and which companies are making significantly less money and might be more prone to near-term investor sentiment or perhaps more vulnerable to a market setback. Although no one can predict the future, many investors believe that hedging their bets with today's proven and profitable technology companies is the best way to reduce your risk, while still taking part in the technology boom. History has shown that those companies with a strong financial position are more likely to emerge from any potential storm with the least amount of damage.

Where's the beef?
What really goes into a company's reported revenue? Just like when you order fast food, when you invest in stocks, make sure you're not getting additives or substitutes. Listen to what the CEO and professional analysts have to say about where a company's revenues come from—and know how they're accounted for.

A Four-Step Checklist for Researching Technology Stocks

We've covered a lot of material to this point; evaluating technology companies on many of these dimensions requires both time and persistence. If you're keen on technology investing, take a few minutes to pass your investment candidate through the following checklist. Although fairly high level, this checklist addresses several key questions that should be reviewed before making an investment.

1. Is the business growing? Your best investment opportunities will have sales growth year over year, of at least 15 percent per year. Sales growth (i.e. revenue) tells a fairly obvious story, namely, that a growing market exists for the company's products and services.

2. Is the business highly profitable? Pre-tax profit margins of 15 percent or better describe a company that likely has a proprietary edge among its competitors. Of course, in the case of development stage Internet companies, any profit may still be a long way off.

3. Does the company make good use of invested capital? A healthy, well-managed company should be able to use existing capital and assets to drive its internal growth. Return-on-equity should be at least 15-20 percent.

4. Is the business reinvesting for the future? R&D (research and development) is the driver here, just as we assume in the growth flow calculations. Sufficient R&D spending shows that management is determined to invest in the future. Total R&D spending should be at least 7 percent of revenues. For younger companies, look for R&D to be even higher.

Will knowing all this information make you a better investor? Maybe not. It might make you smarter, but it won't necessarily make you better. What will make you a better investor will be your consistency, your clarity, your commitment to your plan. Keep your eye on the prize— your financial security and well-being.

CHAPTER 18

Let's Talk
Trends

Technical Analysis:
When The Past is Prologue

echnical analysis has its roots in the theory that where a market index or stock price has gone in the past indicates where it'll go in the future—due largely to the role human behavior plays in determining price. These theories suggest that understanding how investors have reacted, as a group, to certain market conditions is the key to predicting how they'll react in the future under similar conditions.

For example, if the Federal Reserve Board raises interest rates to slow the economy, investors are likely to react negatively, sparking a sell-off in the stock market that drives stock prices down. This can cause more investors to begin selling off, driving prices down farther, until interest rates are slashed and investors start buying again, initiating a rebound.

At the opposite extreme, in a market surge, such as the one that closed out the twentieth century, greed kicks in. (Greed and fear are two of the strongest psychological factors in market prices that technical analysts base their theories on.) As investors saw stock prices going up, more and more of them jumped on the bandwagon, driving the market higher and higher.

Technical analysts try to extrapolate from existing data what the future will bring. They use various types of graphs and tools to interpret future price movements.

Reading Between the Lines

The basic concepts of technical analysis may sound simple, but putting them into practice is another thing altogether. Technical analysis can be complex and confusing, especially to novice investors who may not know what to look for or how to interpret what they see. But you're still reading, so I'll keep explaining. To get you started, I'll introduce you to three key aspects of technical analysis:

1. Trending: Continuous price movement upward or downward over a period of time that indicate the market or security is generally heading in that direction.

2. Oscillation: Short-term price fluctuations within a *trading range* that serve as indicators of turning points in price direction.

3. Patterns: Identifiable shapes formed on a historical price graph that can be used to forecast future price movements.

TURN UP THE VOLUME

Volume signals are one simple tool that analysts use to identify who's in charge —to see whether buyers or sellers are controlling the rise or fall in the price of a security.

Trending

What Is a Trend?

The price action of a stock that is trending can be categorized as trending either up or down (that is, moving generally up or down in price). Range-bound stocks are categorized by price fluctuations that move over time within a narrow band (moving predominately sideways). And non-trending stocks do not move in any clear direction.

When Does a Trend Occur?

An up trend occurs when the price of a market or an individual stock keeps going up, reaching continuously higher highs. When prices keep going down, reaching continuously lower lows, it signals a downtrend. In order to trend, prices do not need to constantly move only up or down, but rather indicate directionally, over time, a consistent upward or downward movement.

Why Do I Care About Trends?

The trend is your friend! Technical analysts try to spot trends because they believe it's much easier to make money in a market or security whose price is trending than in one that's not. Trending is useful for identifying potentially attractive stocks to invest in. Technical analysts use other indicators to identify the best time to invest.

How Do I Spot a Trend?

There are a number of different tools you can use to spot a trend. Moving average data can help identify trends in price direction. To calculate an average, moving average lines plot each day's closing price (in a market or a stock) over a period of time. These averages are connected to establish a trend line—a developing picture of where the price is generally going that can indicate whether and when to buy or sell.

Some traders find moving average graphs to be useful and informative tools for gauging which stocks to take a position in and which stocks to get out of. This is because moving averages can indicate floors that prices are likely not to go below when averages are rising, or ceilings that prices are likely not to go above when averages are falling.

You can use the interaction between price and moving average to map, compare, or contrast moving averages, and draw a bead on the market or a security's general trend. All are available online through E*TRADE or ClearStation (*www.clearstation.com*), an E*TRADE-affiliated investment insight Web site and community focused on helping investors make smarter investment decisions.

- **Simple Moving Average (SMA).** This average line shows the market or a security's moving average over a short period. These average lines respond to each piece of data twice: once when a closing price is factored in, and again when it drops off to be replaced by the latest closing price. This could result in an unreliable buy or sell signal. For example, when a high price is dropped, the moving average will most likely tick down. When the low price is dropped, the moving average would probably tick up, even if the price went up that day, but by an amount smaller than the value that was dropped.

- **Exponential Moving Average (EMA).** This line combines two periods of moving averages in security or market prices: A shorter term (13–20 days) and longer term (50–120 days). Technical analysts believe this is a more reliable indicator of a trend because it weights the latest data and responds faster to changes than a simple moving average.

- **MACD (Moving Average Convergence/Divergence).** This graph compares the interaction of two exponential moving averages—a long-term moving average for 26 days, and a short-term moving average for 12 days—to produce *bullish* and *bearish* signals. The interaction between these averages, or how they converge or diverge, creates the trend line. This line indicates the rate of change in the price and the significance of the change as a signal to buy or sell. By closely watching the MACD, investors can determine whether a stock is currently trending up or down and make an estimation as to whether or not the trend is likely to continue. At ClearStation, you can view trend lines based on MACD (and some other factors) without needing to interpret complicated MACD movements. Green bars above a stock's price chart suggest an uptrend, while red bars suggest a downtrend.

For periods where no bar appears, a stock's price movement does not clearly suggest an up or down trend. Take a look at the DELL price chart (for August 1999 through March 2000) to see color-coded trend lines in action.

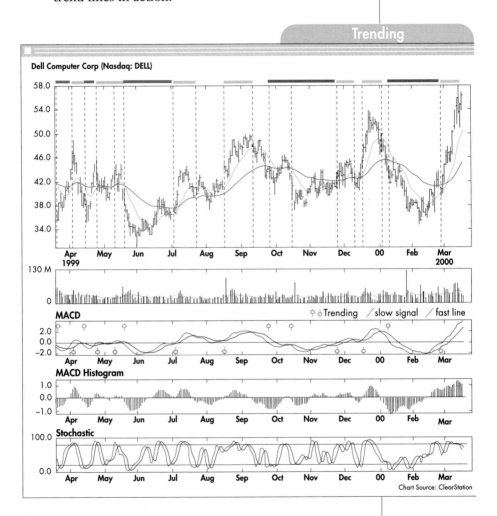

Trending

Dell Computer Corp (Nasdaq: DELL)

Chart Source: ClearStation

Bollinger Bands
Bollinger Bands are another sophisticated diagnostic tool for charting price direction. This data lines chart bands above and below moving averages as yardsticks of market

volatility. A band marks one standard deviation (fluctuation in return) above the security's moving price average, and another marks one standard deviation below this average. The spread between the two bands can indicate the volatility of the market.

Oscillation

What Is Oscillation?

An oscillator compares the current price of a stock to its past trading range. Once you've found a stock you're interested in, oscillators can identify short-term price fluctuations to help you determine whether the current price level is sustainable or on the verge of doing an about-face and heading in the opposite direction.

Why Do I Care About Oscillation?

Oscillators can help you identify entry or exit points (when to buy or sell) by signaling potential turning points in price. They may also indicate a broader, more significant up- or down-trend. Oscillators should be used in conjunction with a trending diagnostic such as MACD to confirm a trend.

How Do I Spot Oscillation?

Stochastic is an oscillator. It compares the current trading price of a security to the trading range over a short period, charting all the back and forth fluctuations during that time. This reveals a pattern that may predict future turning points.

You can see the essential behavioral attributes of stochastic and MACD in the following ClearStation indicator graphs of Oracle (ORCL).

When you're convinced of a trend's integrity, buying on pullbacks often makes sense. Stochastic is a tool to help you identify these opportunities.

Patterns

Why Are Patterns Important?

Patterns are identifiable shapes on an historical price graph. Head and Shoulders. Double Bottom. Ascending Triangle.

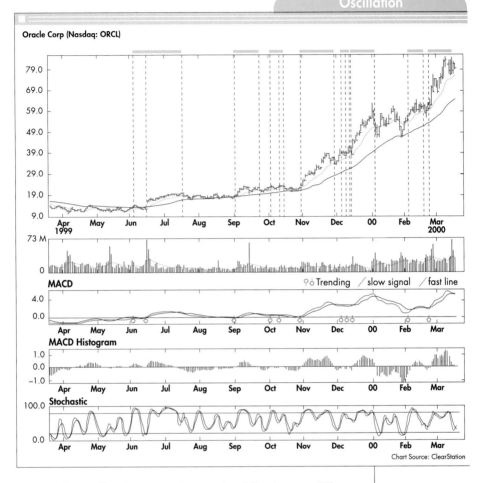

Oracle Corp (Nasdaq: ORCL)

Chart Source: ClearStation

Cup and Handle. Pennant. Support and Resistance. These are some of the better-known patterns that can be identified in the graphs of price activity of certain stocks. Sometimes these patterns can help you forecast the future action of a stock price.

For this initial discussion, let's focus on support and resistance—the ability to identify a distinct trend to the upper and lower limits of buying and selling activity within a certain stock. These patterns may forecast whether a current trend will continue or reverse itself.

How Do I Use Patterns in Support and Resistance?

Support and resistance are price levels. Price support is a level below which a security or market price never seems to fall; price resistance is a level above which the price cannot seem to rise. To create support and resistance lines, you draw a horizontal line connecting across the lowest price levels (identifying support) and another horizontal line connecting across the highest price levels (identifying resistance.) In other words, support and resistance lines respectively appear to serve as floors and ceilings, with the security's price movements bouncing, sometimes wildly, between the two. The strength of each line as a pattern map of future price behavior is determined by how long it's served as the marker of a security's price support or resistance level. The longer it has held, the stronger it is.

The distance between lines is a factor of line strength too. The farther apart they are, the stronger each line is. Finally, volume is part of the mix as well—because the strength of each line increases if trading volume is heavy while price is bouncing around from floor to ceiling.

Support and Resistance

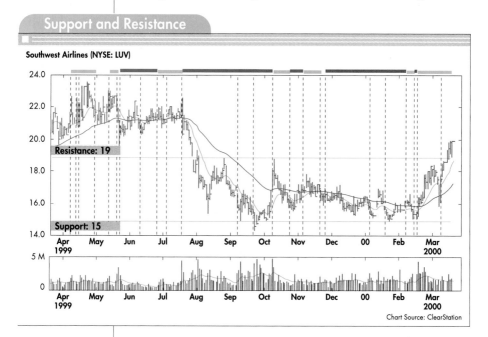

Southwest Airlines (NYSE: LUV)

Resistance: 19

Support: 15

Chart Source: ClearStation

Where Can I See These Patterns?

An example of a stock's support and resistance lines is illustrated in the previous chart for Southwest Airlines (LUV). If a stock's price breaks through an established resistance line, that line often becomes the new support level for that stock. Similarly, if a stock's price falls through a support line, that line will likely become a resistance line.

Intrigued by technical analysis? You should be. It's a powerful tool. It assumes that past price activity, in and of itself, takes into account many key fundamental factors (earnings, management activity, outlook, etc.) and can be a window into future price behavior. Remember that this type of analysis is just one approach that some experienced and informed investors use to analyze the markets and their investments. It is best used in conjunction with all the other analytical tools we've talked about. For more information on technical analysis and some hands-on education, go to *www.clearstation.com/education*.

IPOs and More
Advanced Stuff

As you become more comfortable with online investing, you might want to explore some advanced techniques. These techniques aren't for everybody. But since they've been in the media spotlight recently, I thought it was important to give you a brief introduction to each of these investing trends and a general sense of what they entail.

Three Advanced Investing Styles for the Braveheart Investor

1. Investing in IPOs
2. Day Trading
3. Extended-Hours Trading

Investing in IPOs

Until very recently, individual investors were at a disadvantage when it came to getting shares in an Initial Public Offering (IPO). Traditionally, participation in IPOs—and access to their relatively attractive offering prices—was reserved for big time institutional investors. In the late 1990s, in large part due to the efforts of companies like

E*TRADE, **underwriters** started to become more receptive to the power of the retail market (that's you!) and have started to aim for wider distribution of IPOs, outside the traditional pool of institutional accounts.

When investing in IPOs, the risk *is* significant. The rewards *can be* significant. Note the difference. Although the risk is always significant, the rewards are rarely so. But when they are, they're spectacular, which is part of the appeal of IPOs in the first place.

When a company decides to go public, it hires a lead underwriter to handle the issuing of its stock. The underwriter sets the IPO's price and sells shares to its major customers in advance of the stock trading publicly.

The price the underwriter sets is usually lower than the price where the IPO initially trades publicly. This lower price, called the *IPO discount*, is one of the main attractions of IPOs to investors: The value of their holdings will probably increase when the stock hits the public markets, and could climb even higher in minutes if the stock really takes off. Lead underwriters usually try to price an issue so that the first after-market trade is about 15 percent higher than the IPO discount price, although recently we've seen much more outrageous premiums.

underwriters
Generally, a group of investment banks that are responsible for handling the financing required to transition a company from private to public. Usually one bank leads the rest of the group (the syndicate).

Recent Public Offerings

Some examples of companies that have distributed portions of their Initial Public Offerings to E*TRADE customers.

You say you want to play? You may not be able to. IPO investing is for advanced investors for three reasons.

1. You have to be an experienced investor in order to participate. If you want to participate in an IPO online through a financial service provider such as E*TRADE, you need to complete and pass a suitability profile. This information is used to assess your financial situation and your level of investing experience and whether this is a suitable investment for you. It's also used to determine if there are any relationships that may disqualify you from participating in a particular offering. Your spouse works for the issuing company? That's a no-no. Your daughter, the lawyer, represents an affiliate? That won't fly, either. The SEC wants to be sure there's no possibility of someone having an inside angle.

2. The degree of risk is intense. An IPO is uncharted territory. Unlike a stock that's been trading publicly for some time, IPOs have no track record. What's their past performance? What's the basis for their claims about future growth? How can you follow a trend or analysis if there isn't any history to track? To be an IPO investor, you've got to be rock solid, fearless, and willing to risk all your investment.

3. The number of shares available, and your chances of getting some, may be extremely limited. IPOs have been extremely popular lately—and it always seems there's more demand than supply. Even if you fit all the criteria and submit a conditional offer, there's no guarantee you're going to get any shares.

Given all that, how do investors evaluate an IPO's quality? There are some indicators that can help an IPO investor gauge the degree of risk:

Spin-offs. The issuing company, which has no track record, might be a major spin-off or large subsidiary of an established parent company. Both the parent company and the division being spun off might have long (even successful) track records. On the other hand, the spin-off may be a brand-new and unproven entity.

The IPO's prospectus. Investors pay close attention to key sections of an IPO's prospectus, which can be easily accessed online. Where did the company get its money? How is it spending it? What are the identified business problems that might be considered risk factors? IPOs are required to disclose expectations of having to issue additional shares in the future to raise more money (a possible warning bell to investors that the initial offering is insufficient to meet the company's capital needs). All these factors are guidelines to the chances of success.

After-market performance. How has the underwriter done in the past? After-market performance tracks the success the IPO underwriter has had in bringing other IPOs to market. Basically, many investors evaluate each new offering based on the underwriter's batting average.

E*TRADE's IPO Center lists current and completed IPOs distributed to our customers from a variety of sectors, from health care and consumer products to industrials and technologies.

The preliminary prospectus of each available public offering (some are **secondary offerings**) is available online for review by anyone. Active investors can also get a ranking of various underwriters' track records from our after-market performance monitoring site.

As with any investment, market news, commentary, and Web discussions can also be valuable resources for IPO information. E*TRADE links investors to each resource from our IPO Center.

At E*TRADE, once you have determined an IPO is an appropriate investment for you, have completed your suitability profile, and have been approved for participation in a particular public offering, you can then place a conditional offer online. This tells us you'd like to buy a specific number of shares of a particular IPO at a given price, with a specific limit. But a conditional offer does not guarantee that you will actually be able to purchase shares at the

> **secondary offering**
> A follow-on to an initial public offering. The public sale of previously issued stock held by the company or large investors.

offering price (or even at your limit price).

IPOs are often in very high demand, and shares are limited. All underwriters and selling group members, including E*TRADE, can only allocate the shares they have available. E*TRADE is unique in that we try to give the opportunity to participate in each IPO we participate in to as many investors as possible, using a proprietary distribution algorithm.

If you're successful in purchasing IPO shares, think twice about turning them over quickly to generate a fast gain. This strategy is called flipping and could result in penalties imposed by your broker, who may limit your access to IPO shares in the future. E*TRADE strongly discourages flipping. We don't fine you for it or even require you to hold onto your IPO shares for a set period of time before selling them as some brokers do, but we do discourage the practice.

Day Trading

All day traders are active traders, but not all active traders are day traders.

Day traders are investors who may not hold a position (own a security) for even as long as overnight. In general, day traders seek frequent small gains and occasional big ones. Unlike the average investor who buys and holds a security possibly until retirement, a day trader might buy and hold only until the price of the security goes up, say, just $\frac{1}{8}$ of a point.

Day traders tend to focus on just a handful of stocks, buy large numbers of shares, and sell after very small movements in price in order to make fast money. They're the ultimate short-term investors. Again, it's not for the conservative, inexperienced, or faint-of-heart.

Because the risks involved are as great as the potential

rewards, day trading requires a high level of skill. Day traders need eyes and ears that are finely tuned to every market nuance, hardy nerves, and an industrial-strength "no guts, no glory" attitude that average investors—even active traders—might consider daredevil.

Day traders have twin passions: speed and information. Because they aren't concerned with macrotrends but instead base their decisions on short-term probabilities, they live and breathe real-time quotes, charts, and graphs, and they have voracious appetites for the latest market news and rumors. They don't concern themselves with many of the research and analysis tools E*TRADE makes available to the average online investor. They're interested only in the tools that focus most heavily on their need for speed.

For example, it's unlikely that day traders ever give historical charts more than a passing glance. Instead, they focus on intraday charts, which track security price fluctuations incrementally in real-time throughout a trading day, so they can time their moves with more precision.

ClearStation's *Three-Point Investing* approach mirrors the experience of "the trading floor" by providing access to key fundamental and technical resources and discussions. ClearStation generates charts and technical analysis that may benefit day traders by synthesizing mathematical data into visual cues on graphs used to identify and follow a security's short-term trend. Day traders place great emphasis on these cues because their bread and butter depends not only on being able to spot a trend but knowing how long to ride it and just when to benefit from short-term price movements.

Access to deeper price data such as Nasdaq Level II Quotes, which E*TRADE makes available to our most active investors, is also of paramount importance to the speed- and information-driven day trader. Level II Quotes show the volume of shares lined up at different prices for a particular security. This information gives day traders a

E*TRADE PULSE

Symbol	Last Sale	Day Chg	%Chg	Last Size	High	Low	Bid Price	Ask Price	Daily Volume	PD.Close	Last Tim
YHOO	$167^1{}_2$	$1^{19}{}_{54}$	0.78	500	$171^5{}_8$	$159^1{}_4$	$167^1{}_2$	$167^9{}_{16}$	7836600	$166^{13}{}_{64}$	15:55:0

Story | Symbol Search | Analytics | Mkt View | Download | **Level II** | Preferences | About | List Management | Clear List

YHOO   Last Sale **$167^1{}_2$**   Daily Change **$1^{19}{}_{64}$**   Last Time **15:55**
Yahoo Inc   Daily Volume **7836600**   Low **$159^1{}_4$**   High **$171^5{}_8$**

	BID	133	174	ASK	
	HRZG	$167^1{}_2$	$167^9{}_{16}$	**INCA**	

BID				ASK			
HRZG	15:53	1	$167^1{}_2$	$167^9{}_{16}$	12	15:55	**INCA**
NITE	15:53	10	$167^1{}_4$	$167^{11}{}_{16}$	10	15:54	ISLD
MASH	15:54	1	$167^3{}_{16}$	$167^3{}_{16}$	4	15:54	FBCO
SLKC	15:52	1	167		1	15:54	FLTT
ISLD	15:54	1		$167^{15}{}_{16}$	1	15:54	MWSE
ARCA	15:55	20	$166^3{}_4$	168	1	15:54	BRUT
DEAN	15:54	1	$166^5{}_8$	$168^3{}_8$	1	15:47	SWST
REDI	15:54	10	$166^1{}_2$	$168^1{}_2$	10	15:53	NITE
MADF	15:52	1	$165^7{}_8$		5	15:55	**ARCA**
FBCO	15:54	1	$165^{13}{}_{16}$		2	15:54	DEAN
INCA	15:55	5	$165^3{}_4$		1	15:52	MADF

Symbol	Last Sale	Day Chg
LU	$55^9{}_{16}$	$2^{11}{}_{16}$
AOL	$60^5{}_{16}$	2
TOM	$11^3{}_4$	$-^1{}_4$
DAL	$46^3{}_4$	$^1{}_4$
PFE	$33^1{}_4$	$-^3{}_4$
ORCL	$61^9{}_{16}$	$-1^1{}_2$
AMZN	$68^5{}_{16}$	$-2^1{}_8$
YHOO	$167^1{}_2$	$1^{19}{}_{64}$
MSFT	$94^3{}_8$	$^1{}_8$
DELL	$42^3{}_8$	1
CSCO	$137^1{}_4$	$-1^3{}_8$
INTC	$114^1{}_4$	$5^3{}_{16}$

February 24, 2000 3:55 PM ET   **Real-time quotes**

sense of the level of pricing support for a security in the short term. Assuming that their sense is keen, it can be instrumental in timing the market correctly.

Extended-Hours Trading

As I'm writing this, the NYSE, AMEX, and NASDAQ are open for business from 9:30 A.M. to 4:00 P.M. eastern time Monday through Friday. When was the last time any of us worked those hours?

Historically, individual investors could trade U.S. securities only during these hours, unless they accessed foreign exchanges listing U.S. securities that operate in a different time zone.

Recently, the growth and demands of online investing have resulted in changes that allow individual investors to trade stocks through systems called *Electronic Communications Networks* (ECNs). ECNs match buy/sell orders and execute them after regular market hours. More and more, ECNs are also operating during market hours.

After-hours trading has been in existence for a decade but was available only to institutional investors. Now, online retail investors have direct access to after-hours trading via ECNs through services such as E∗TRADE, giving you the opportunity to place orders and have them executed outside market hours.

What's the advantage? It lets advanced investors act on market news made after the markets close, pursue hot leads as soon as they come in, and maybe seize an opportunity before others wake up to it. There are several downsides to playing the market this way that may increase risk. The major risk to the individual investor is the lack of *liquidity*. The other is *volatility*.

During regular market hours, the **market makers** and exchanges execute trades almost every millisecond. This is good for investors because it tends to make the spreads between securities' bid and ask prices very tight.

Take a regular-hours quarter point spread of a bid of 35 and an ask of 35¼ on the price of a stock—not unusual in normal trading hours. But because there's much less activity going on in the after-hours markets, spreads tend to become bigger—and that same stock might have a bid of 32 and an ask of 38 on the price.

Think about that from an investing point of view. As an investor, you sell at the bid price and buy at the asking price. Dealers (*market makers*), however, buy at the bid and sell at the ask. So, the risk to individual investors of trading after hours is that there is fundamentally less liquidity the more the spread broadens.

market maker
A professional trader on the Nasdaq system who maintains firm bid and ask prices on a specific security and is ready to buy and sell round lots of that security.

Now It's Up to You

Every time you increase your information and knowledge, you create a new beginning. It's a continual process of learning. The more you learn, the more you do. That's what life is all about.

It's my wish that everyone become more informed and more educated so that each of us can make the difference in our own lives. Now is the time to make that difference for yourself and for your financial future.

Breathe In, Breathe Out

As we go to press with this book, dramatic shifts are happening in the marketplace. On April 3, 2000, just one month after new all-time highs in the Nasdaq, the index violently plummeted following a ruling on the Microsoft antitrust case. Microsoft stock, along with many other Nasdaq stocks, brought the index down over 900 points within just two days of trading. Nobody predicted the spontaneous increase early in the millennium and nobody predicted the spontaneous and severe fall.

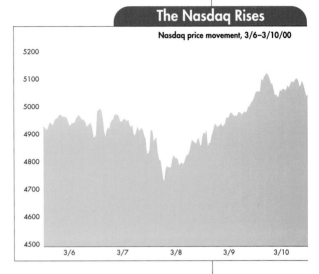

No matter what the outcome, just remember it's always those people armed with knowledge, information and access who weather best through these storms. During the crash of 1987, critical, real-time information was available to only a few individuals inside financial institutions. Now through your PC, telephone, television (and more!) real-time information on what's happening, and why, is available to anyone with access to any of these channels and a little knowledge of where to

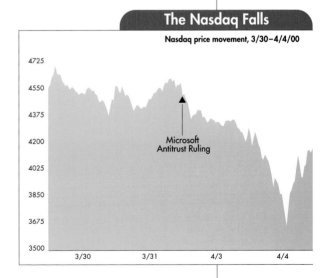

look and what to look for. Although information is no guarantee of success, it can make the difference between a rash decision and an informed one.

Talking the Talk

10-Q • A quarterly financial report submitted by public companies to the SEC (Securities and Exchange Commission).

10-K • An annual financial report submitted by public companies to the SEC. It provides a comprehensive overview of the business.

12b-1 fee • A fee indirectly charged to shareholders of certain mutual funds for the fund's marketing costs.

account equity • The total amount of assets (cash and fully-owned securities) in an account minus any liabilities (amounts borrowed and still owed).

all-or-none (AON) order • An order to buy or sell all your shares of a security at one time, or none at all. Execution of AON orders have the lowest priority in the marketplace, and typically must be for a minimum of 300 shares. A *market* order cannot be placed this way.

annualized earnings • The equivalent annual return on an investment calculated by multiplying the amount earned in a given period (weekly, monthly, etc.) by the number of pay periods a year. For example, if a mutual fund earns 1 percent in a month, its annualized return would be 12 percent (1 percent x 12 months).

annualized seven-day yield • The annual return on an investment expressed as a percentage of the amount invested. It assumes that the investment's performance throughout the year is the same as its performance over a particular seven-day period.

annual report • Statement of a company or mutual fund's financial picture (earnings, assets, liabilities) and other corporate data issued yearly to shareholders, and available, in most cases, on the company's Web site.

ask price • The price a seller is willing to accept for a security. From an investor's point of view, the lowest market price at which the security can be purchased. Also known as the offering price.

ask size • The number of shares available at the ask price.

assets under management • The total of all investments and cash making up one or more portfolios managed by a mutual fund.

bid price • The price a buyer is willing to pay for a security. From an investor's point of view, the highest market price at which an investor can sell a security.

bid size • The number of shares available at the bid price.

buying power • In a margin account, the maximum dollar amount of marginable securities that the account holder can purchase or sell short without having to deposit additional funds.

call • An options contract with the right to buy a specific number of shares of a stock at a specified price (the strike price) on or before a specific expiration date, regardless of the underlying stock's current market price.

call provision • Contractual right of a stock or bond issuer to retire its preferred stock, or pay off its bond debt before maturity, for a premium price paid to the holder.

clearing • Process of reconciling accounts following a securities transaction.

combination • Method of investing in options in which calls and puts have different expiration dates, fixed prices, or both.

commission • Fees paid to a brokerage/financial service provider to execute a transaction or to manage an investment portfolio.

compounding • The growth in income of an original investment coupled with reinvested earnings.

cover or buy to cover • To buy shares of a security to offset a *short* position.

covered call • Selling a *call option* while owning the same number of shares represented by the option in the underlying stock.

covered put • Selling a put while holding a *short* position in the underlying stock.

current yield • The rate of return on a bond if it were bought or sold today.

day order • Order to buy or sell a security only on the market day it is entered, or, if the order is entered when the market is closed, on the following trading day only. All market orders are day orders. Also called a "good-for-day" order.

dividend • A distribution of a portion of a company's earnings to its shareholders in cash or stock.

dollar cost averaging • Averaging the cost per share of a particular security by investing a fixed sum regularly.

earnings per share (EPS) • Net income per share of a company's common stock, after deducting taxes, depreciation allowances, potential losses, payments to holders of preferred stock and bonds, and other costs.

earnings report • Quarterly or annual statement issued by a public company reporting its revenues, expenses, and profit for that period. Also called a profit and loss (P&L) statement.

equity percentage • In a margin account, this percentage is calculated by dividing the market value of cash and fully-owned securities versus the market value of the amount owed on margin (borrowed fund).

exercise an option • To buy or sell a call or put option by the expiration date on the options contract.

good-until-cancelled • Also known as good 'til cancelled (GTC). An order which remains open until it is executed, cancelled or expires (at E*TRADE open orders expire after 60 days).

hedge • To reduce risk in an investment by offsetting it with another investment.

high • The highest price at which a security has traded during the current (or most recent) trading session.

inception date • The day on which a mutual fund began selling shares to the public.

in-the-money • When an option's current market price is above the strike price of a call, or below the strike price of a put. An in-the-money option would produce a profit, if exercised.

leverage • A means of minimizing your own cash outlay by investing with borrowed funds (i.e., through a margin account). It also refers to the potential to generate a proportionally greater amount of return from an initial investment.

limit order • Order to buy a security at or below a specified price, or to sell at or above a specified price.

load • An additional fee added by certain mutual funds to the purchase and/or sale price of a fund. Mutual funds are often categorized by the types of fees the fund company charges you for buying or selling shares.

— **back-end load fund.** A fund that charges a fee when you sell your shares; this fee may decrease the longer you've held onto your shares.

Also called contingent deferred sales charges (CDSC).

— **front-end load fund.** A fund that charges a fee for purchasing shares.

— **level-load fund.** A fund that charges an annual fee for marketing costs (a12b-1 fee).

— **no-load fund.** A fund that charges no fee for buying or selling shares. Although with no-load funds, the fund does not charge a fee, the financial service provider may charge a commission to execute the transaction.

long call • Buying a call option.

long put • Buying a put option.

lot • The quantity of shares in which stocks are bought or sold.

— **odd lot.** A quantity of shares not divisible by 100.

— **round lot.** Multiple of 100 shares.

low • The lowest price at which a security has traded during the current (or most recent) trading session.

margin • Borrowing money from a financial service provider (brokerage or bank) to purchase securities.

margin call • A Federal Reserve Board and financial service provider requirement that you deposit additional funds or sell some of your holdings to increase the equity in your margin account if it has fallen below the minimum.

margin debit • The amount of money borrowed from a financial service provider.

market order • Order to execute a purchase or sale for the best price available at the time the order is received.

NBBO • Short for "national best bid and offer", a requirement that a brokerage guarantee customers the best price available when buying or selling securities.

out-of-the-money • When an option's current market price is below the strike price of a call or above the strike price of a put.

P/E ratio • Price-to-earnings ratio, the current price of a stock divided by its earnings the previous year.

position • Your financial stake in a given security or financial instrument.

put • An options contract with the right to sell a security at a specified exercise price on or before a specific expiration date.

return • The earnings, or yield, you receive from your investment.

sell short • Selling shares of a security in the belief that their price will drop and you'll be able to repay the loan at a profit by buying the shares back at the lower price.

settlement date • The date when payment must be made for a security transaction (either to the investor or the financial service provider), or when certificates must be received by the financial service provider. Settlement dates are usually three business days following transactions, but with options, government bonds and Treasury bills, settlement dates are the next business day following execution of the order.

short call • Selling a call option that you don't already own.

short put • Selling a put option.

spread • A position consisting of two options, with one being written (sold) based on one that is held. A spread position with a put and a call is called a combination.

statement • A record of your transaction activity provided by your financial service provider.

stop limit order • An order that is triggered when the stop price is reached but can only be executed at the limit price.

stop order • An order to buy or sell a security if and when its current market price reaches the price you specify. This becomes a trigger to execute the order at the going market price (it may or may not be the same as the stop price).

straddle • Buying both a call and a put on the same stock—most often with the same exercise price and expiration date. Purpose is to profit from expected volatility.

street name • Term applied to securities held in the name of the financial service provider (on behalf of the actual owner). Holding securities in street name can make a sales transaction easier to complete.

strike price • Fixed price of an option.

ticker symbol • Standard abbreviation used to refer to a stock when placing orders or conducing research.

trade date • The day a security is bought or sold.

writer • A seller of options contracts.

Bibliography
& E-Contact Sites

Want to know more? There are plenty of good books and Web sites out there. Here is just a sample of some I've found helpful.

Books

Every Investors Guide to High-Tech Stocks and Mutual Funds: Proven Strategies for Picking High-Growth Winners, Michael Murphy, (Broadway Books, 1999)

Getting Started in Options, 3rd Edition, Michael C. Thomsett, (John Wiley & Sons, 1997)

The Green Magazine Guide to Personal Finance, Ken Kurson, (Doubleday, 1998)

The Intelligent Investor, Benjamin Graham, (Harper Business, 1985)

How to Invest in E-Commerce Stocks, Bill Burnham, (McGraw Hill, 1999)

The Millionaire Next Door: The Surprising Secrets of America's Wealthy, Thomas J. Stanley and William S. Danko, (Longstreet Press, 1996)

The Motley Fool Investment Guide: How the Fools Beat Wall Street's Wise Men and How You Can Too, David Gardner and Tom Gardner, (Fireside, 1997)

The 9 Steps to Financial Freedom, Suze Orman, (Crown, 1997)

One Up On Wall Street, Peter Lynch, (Penguin USA, 1990)

A Random Walk Down Wall Street, Burton G. Malkiel, (W.W. Norton, 1996)

24 Essential Lessons for Investment Success, William J. O'Neil, (McGraw Hill, 2000)

The Wall Street Journal Guide to Understanding Money & Investing, Kenneth M. Morris, et al, (Fireside, 1999)

The Wealthy Barber, Updated 3rd Edition, David Chilton, (Prima, 1998)

What Works on Wall Street, James P. O'Shaughnessy, (McGraw Hill, 1997)

Your Money or Your Life, Joe Dominguez and Vicky Robin, (Penguin, 1999)

Web Sites

American Association of Individual Investors
www.aaii.com

The Chicago Board Options Exchange
www.cboe.com

ClearStation
www.clearstation.com

CNBC
www.cnbc.com

CNET
www.cnet.com

CNNfn
www.cnnfn.com

Edgar Online
edgar.disclosure.com/ea

E*TRADE
www.etrade.com

Free Edgar
www.freeedgar.com

Gomez Advisors
www.gomez.com

Industry Standard
www.thestandard.com

Investorama
www.investorama.com

IPO Central
www.ipocentral.com

Motley Fool
www.fool.com

MSN MoneyCentral
moneycentral.msn.com

Nasdaq
www.nasdaq.com

National Association of Securities Dealers
www.nasd.com

The New York Stock Exchange
www.nyse.com

The New York Times
www.nytimes.com

OnlineInvestor.com
www.onlineinvestor.com

Securities and Exchange Commission
www.sec.gov

SmartMoney
www.smartmoney.com

Tax and Accounting Sites Directory
www.taxsites.com

TheStreet.com
www.thestreet.com

The Wall Street Journal Interactive
www.wsj.com

Stay in Touch

Investing online doesn't mean you have to go it alone. E*TRADE provides a comprehensive online Learning and Service Center to answer your questions and help you get started. And our Knowledge Center is a valuable source for more in-depth learning on a wide range of personal finance topics. To get started, just visit our Web site at **www.etrade.com**.

If you have additional comments and questions about our products, services, or any other online investing issue, you can also:

E-mail Us:

service@etrade.com

Call Us:

1-800-STOCKS5 (1-800-786-2575)
24 hours a day, seven days a week

Write Us:

E*TRADE Securities, Inc.
P.O. Box 9206
Boston, MA 02205-9891

Acknowledgements

Three people were instrumental in bringing my ideas and this book to life. Steve Lance (a new and great friend) of Unconventional Wisdom, who provided vital editorial input along with candid commentary, nostalgic musings and new age accessories. Pam Kramer, my alter-ego at E✴TRADE, who led and managed the overall development of this project, contributed a significant portion of six months of her life to making this book "right" for our readers. And Brigitte VanBaelen, who delivered valuable insights and scheduling expertise to ensure production deadlines were met.

Special thanks go to several individuals who dedicated many hours of research and editorial assistance. Notable contributions were made by Warren C. Stankiewicz and Jarred Cluff at E✴TRADE and Jeff Woll, Norman Siegel, Kelly Monaghan and Carole Schweid at Unconventional Wisdom.

A number of people generously offered their time and insight by reviewing the manuscript or portions of it. They are Scott Appleby, Erin Burke, Dan Case, James Cramer, Kevin Delo, Patrick Di Chiro, Bob Emery, Amy Errett, Ron Fischer, Richard Fishman, Dale Forman, Jerry Gramaglia, Frank Gutierrez, Kyle Kelly, Josh Levine, Kathy Levinson, Kathleen Magill, Mike McGee, Lenny Mendonca, Stevan Noceti, Marco Pellini, Jeff Perrone, Steve Richards, Mark Schoonbrood, Todd Stern, Lester Thurow, Cassia van der Hoof Holstein, Rob Vaughn and Susan Wolfrom.

Essential legal and regulatory review was led by Ted Theophilos with heroic efforts from Henry Carter, Steve Gatti and Shanti Fishman. Without them, this book really would not have been possible.

At Harper Collins, Adrian (yes, it is done) Zackheim, Greg Chaput and Lisa Berkowitz offered their valuable input and patience throughout the process.

Victoria Pohlmann created a beautiful and very functional design that was expertly executed by Janet Mumford at i4 Design and Philip Dunn at the Book Laboratory.

Finally, special thanks to Tami and Suzanne Renée who gave me the space to be my usual intense self while taking on yet another all consuming project.

About the Author

Only one person could have the courage to tell the truth about how you CAN take on those who say you can't run your own money, and then show you how easy it can be to do. Christos is that person. He has empowered more people to get smart about money than any individual in this era. He's done it by showing people everyday what he knew all along: you can figure out these financial markets and you can beat the pros at their own game.

As a hedge fund manager for these last two decades, I have often wondered what would happen to the money-running profession if people were to take control their own pocketbooks. I always knew the real secret of professional money management: That we, the pros, can never do as well as you, the amateurs, if you put your minds to it, because we don't know your risk tolerance and your cares and wants as you do. We don't know your tax situation and your family situation. We try to empathize with your hopes and dreams, but ultimately those are yours not ours. I have always figured that one day, many money managers would be put out of business by you, the individual, with our craft becoming a niche business devoted only to those too time-consumed to take care of it themselves.

Christos, as self-made and self-directed at they come, understands this better than anyone. Before the Net, do-it-yourselfers, however, didn't stand a chance against the pros. Now all of that has changed, with instant information at your fingertips courtesy the Net. As recently as five years ago, I had to pay hundreds of thousands of dollars a year for the same information as I can get now from sites like Power E*TRADE.

But there are still millions upon millions of people who are scared or intimidated or don't know they can do it themselves better than the pros. That's where Christos comes in. He has always had the faith and the passion that the individual could dominate his or her finances. You put his pioneer vision together with the Net, and you have a revolution on your hands. With this book Christos has given the revolution a manifesto that anyone, young or old, wealthy or soon-to-be, can learn from and devour.

On a personal note, as someone who has tried for years to level the playing field for the smaller investor, Christos is a genuine hero of mine. When I first interviewed him on CNBC, I didn't know much about him, but I remember telling my partner after the interview "There's a guy I want in my foxhole when the shooting starts." Only after I had met him and had gotten to learn the "Christos Story" did I know that, during the Vietnam War, Christos received the Bronze Star for valor while single-handedly wiping out an enemy machine gun nest while serving with the legendary 101st Airborne. Most managers try to simulate or imagine combat situations as they battle daily to make their companies great. For Christos, the lessons were all too real. They have helped mold Christos into a competitor who knows more about giving and individual power than any other exec I have ever come across.

As a hedge fund manager, I make giant bets on companies everyday. When people ask me how I choose those stocks, I always tell them "I look at the management. Would I want to work with them? Would I want to be led by them? Would I believe in them and walk through fire for them? Would I trust them with my financial life?" In the end only a handful measure up to that standard. Christos is at the top of that list. I am proud to call him a friend and a fellow warrior in the never-ending battle to give people the tools and wisdom they need to dominate their own financial world.

—James J. Cramer, Co-founder, TheStreet.com

Christos M. Cotsakos is chairman of the board and chief executive officer of E*TRADE Group, Inc. Prior to joining E*TRADE, Christos served as co-chief executive officer as well as a president, chief operating officer and director at AC Nielsen. He also enjoyed 19 years with Federal Express Corporation where he held a number of senior executive positions.

Christos serves on the board of directors of several leading-edge technology companies in both the public and private sector. A decorated Vietnam veteran, Christos served as a fire team leader with the B Company 2nd Battalion, 501st Infantry, 101st Airborne Division. He received a BA (cum laude) from William Paterson University, an MBA (summa cum laude) from Pepperdine University, and is currently a Ph.D. candidate in the field of economics at the University of London.

Christos has been the recipient of several industry awards and recognitions including:

- "The E-Establishment: The Top 50 Technology Leaders" by *Vanity Fair* (April 2000)
- "The Financial Online Elite" by *Institutional Investor* (April 2000 - September 1997)
- "The Powerful Wall Street Pioneers" by *The Wall Street Journal* (December 1999)
- "The Elite 100" by *Upside Magazine* (December 1999 - December 1998)
- "The 50 Most Important People Shaping Technology Today" by *Time Digital* (October 1999)
- "The e.biz 25. The Most Influential People In Electronic Business" by *Business Week* (September 1999)
- "Power 50 - The Most Influential People in Financial Services" by *Ticker Magazine* (June 1999 - June 1998)
- "The 25 Most Influential Personalities in Financial Services" by *American Banker* (May 1999)
- "Entrepreneur of the Year Award" for the USA (November 1998) and California (June 1998) by the Entrepreneur of the Year Institute.
- "Top 50 Cyber Elite" by *Time Digital* (October 1998)
- "The New Entrepreneurial Elite" by *Inc. Magazine* (December 1997)
- "Top 10 Visionary CEO's" by *Communications Week* (February1997)
- "Thirty Who Matter in Technology" by *Forbes ASAP* (October 1996)

Christos is donating all proceeds from this book to help bridge the digital divide through education and access.

Index